Life Itself is an Art

PSYCHOANALYTIC HORIZONS

Psychoanalysis is unique in being at once a theory and a therapy, a method of critical thinking and a form of clinical practice. Now in its second century, this fusion of science and humanism derived from Freud has outlived all predictions of its demise. **Psychoanalytic Horizons** evokes the idea of a convergence between realms as well as the outer limits of a vision. Books in the series test disciplinary boundaries and will appeal to scholars and therapists who are passionate not only about the theory of literature, culture, media, and philosophy but also, above all, about the real life of ideas in the world.

Series Editors
Esther Rashkin, Mari Ruti, and Peter L. Rudnytsky

Advisory Board
Salman Akhtar, Doris Brothers, Aleksandar Dimitrijevic, Lewis Kirshner, Humphrey Morris, Hilary Neroni, Dany Nobus, Lois Oppenheim, Donna Orange, Peter Redman, Laura Salisbury, Alenka Zupančič

Volumes in the Series

Life Itself Is an Art

The Life and Work of
Erich Fromm

Rainer Funk
Translated from German by Susan Kassouf

BLOOMSBURY ACADEMIC
NEW YORK • LONDON • OXFORD • NEW DELHI • SYDNEY

BLOOMSBURY ACADEMIC
Bloomsbury Publishing Inc
1385 Broadway, New York, NY 10018, USA
50 Bedford Square, London, WC1B 3DP, UK

BLOOMSBURY, BLOOMSBURY ACADEMIC and the Diana logo are trademarks of
Bloomsbury Publishing Plc

First published in the United States of America 2019

Copyright © Rainer Funk, 2019
First published in German by Herder Verlag

Cover design by Alice Marwick
Cover portrait of Erich Fromm, 1980, photographer: Thea Goldman © Rainer Funk

All rights reserved. No part of this publication may be reproduced or transmitted in
any form or by any means, electronic or mechanical, including photocopying,
recording, or any information storage or retrieval system, without prior permission
in writing from the publishers.

Bloomsbury Publishing Inc does not have any control over, or responsibility for, any
third-party websites referred to or in this book. All internet addresses given in this
book were correct at the time of going to press. The author and publisher regret
any inconvenience caused if addresses have changed or sites have ceased to
exist, but can accept no responsibility for any such changes.

Library of Congress Cataloging-in-Publication Data
Names: Funk, Rainer, author. | Kassouf, Susan (Susan Margaret), translator.
Title: Life itself is an art : the life and work of Erich Fromm / Rainer Funk;
translated from German by Susan Kassouf.
Other titles: Leben selbst ist eine Kunst. English
Description: New York : Bloomsbury Academic, 2019. | Series: Psychoanalytic
horizons | Translation of: Das Leben selbst ist eine Kunst : Einfèuhrung in Leben
und Werk von Erich Fromm. | Includes bibliographical references and index.
Identifiers: LCCN 2019007915 (print) | LCCN 2019011476 (ebook) |
ISBN 9781501351464 (ePub) | ISBN 9781501351471 (ePDF) |
ISBN 9781501351457 (hardback) |
ISBN 9781501351440 (pbk.)
Subjects: LCSH: Fromm, Erich, 1900–1980. | Psychoanalysts–Germany–Biography. |
Psychoanalysts–United States–Biography.
Classification: LCC BF109.F76 (ebook) | LCC BF109.F76 F855 2019 (print) |
DDC 150.19/5092 [B] –dc23
LC record available at https://lccn.loc.gov/2019007915

ISBN: HB: 978-1-5013-5145-7
PB: 978-1-5013-5144-0
ePDF: 978-1-5013-5147-1
eBook: 978-1-5013-5146-4

Series: Psychoanalytic Horizons

Typeset by RefineCatch Limited, Bungay, Suffolk

To find out more about our authors and books visit www.bloomsbury.com
and sign up for our newsletters.

Contents

Figures

Preface

Not only medicine, engineering, and painting are arts; living itself is an art—in fact, the most important and at the same time the most difficult and complex art to be practiced by man. Its object is not this or that specialized performance, but the performance of living, the process of developing into that which one is potentially. In the art of living, man is both the artist and the object of his art; he is the sculptor and the marble; the physician and the patient.

Man for Himself, 1947a, pp. 17–18

These sentences from Erich Fromm's book *Man for Himself* are foundational. They signal a view of humanity that reflects the unique conditions of human life, in contrast to other life forms. Because of the way man's brain developed, he has been endowed with a consciousness of himself and with the capacity to imagine reality independently of sensory stimuli.[1] These neurobiological characteristics mean not only that man *can* shape his own life, but also that he *must* shape it.

The *necessity* of an art of living expresses itself through particular psychic needs, specifically the need to relate to reality, to other people, and to oneself. The *possibility* of an art of living is manifested in the different ways that people can relate to themselves, to each other, to the natural world, to work, or to reality: mindfully, calculatingly, lovingly, patronizingly, contemptuously, appreciatively, exploitatively, caringly, etc. Humans are capable of every possibility, but not every possibility is conducive to their personal well-being and the well-being of society. For to flourish as a human being therefore depends upon which possibilities are realized, and whether or not the conditions of living impede or even thwart certain possibilities. In addition to these sociopolitical and ethical dimensions, there is still another feature of

---

[1]   As Fromm tended to use "man" to describe people in his writings, thereby indicating both sexes with the masculine form, I keep this usage in the quotations as well as elsewhere.

living as an art, or the art of living, as Fromm understands it: the goal is not to know how life functions, in the way that self-help books impart information about a certain sort of expertise and its application. For man, life itself is an art, because what allows man and society to flourish can only be recognized by the transformative effects of the art of living.

The following introduction to Fromm attempts to do justice to the foundational idea that life itself is an art by exploring the connections between his life and his work. The theoretical aspects of Fromm's thought are preceded by biographical sections that link his theoretical insights with his life history. This introduction to the life and work of Fromm thus reveals itself to be an introduction to the art of living according to Fromm.

The uniqueness of Fromm's psychology lies in his social-psychoanalytic approach in which the individual is understood primarily as a social being. The demands of the market and communal life are thereby reflected in a particular psychic structural formation that Fromm called *social character*. Yet, the individual is only conscious of socially generated impulses to the extent that these impulses correspond to social and individual ideals. For Fromm, there is not only an individual unconscious, but also a social unconscious as well as social repression. This book aims to provide interested readers as well as students with an accessible yet still precise and comprehensive introduction to the life's work of Erich Fromm.

I would like to thank Dr. Susan Kassouf for translating this book into English. She is not merely familiar with psychoanalytic theories but also gifted with a nuanced sense of language that has ideally equipped her to convey Fromm's humanistic ideas.

And I would like to express my gratitude to Professor Peter Rudnytsky, coeditor of the Psychoanalytic Horizons series, and to Haaris Naqvi, Editorial Director of Bloomsbury Academic, for their interest in Erich Fromm's life and work and for their great support in making it possible to publish this book.

Rainer Funk
Tübingen
October 2018

Figure 1 Fromm, 1970, by Liss Goldring. © Lit Fromm Estate.

Introduction

Direct Encounter

On September 1, 1972, I rang the bell at the entrance to the apartment building Casa La Monda in Muralto, near Locarno, Switzerland, and took the tiny elevator to the fifth floor. I had no idea that this first personal encounter with Erich Fromm would be the beginning of a life-changing relationship for me. Having just begun work on a doctoral dissertation in theological ethics, I was determined to find out how Fromm, a self-avowed non-theist, justified his humanistic ethics without believing in an entity that transcended the human being and human thought.

Everything that I had been taught up to that point and everything that I had learned, tried, and experienced in the previous twenty-nine years had been centered around education and ideas. I was absolutely convinced that this was the way to master life, even my personal, social, moral, and religious life. My educational goal was to comprehend and intellectually to preserve what made us human. After Auschwitz, I was equally certain that we could only place our hopes in humanity if it were protected against failure by something that transcended it. Fromm's humanistic justification of ethics struck me as dubious—too trusting and naive. In my initial letter to him of August 1, 1972, I had already intimated that his humanism would clearly be "the starting point for a constructive debate."

The elevator finally arrived on the fifth floor. When the doors opened, I looked straight at Erich Fromm. He was standing in the doorway of his apartment, regarding me in a friendly and expectant way. I took two steps toward him and greeted the 72-year-old stiffly with the formal address "Professor." He shook hands with me and facing me, replied, "Guten Tag, Herr Funk." In the hallway behind him Annis, his American wife two years his junior, appeared. She was a head taller than he, and greeted me in an almost incomprehensible Southern drawl: "How are you?" Her facial expression revealed curiosity, with an amicable but slightly skeptical smile.

Fromm invited me to join him in his study. My first impression was of the breathtaking view of Lake Maggiore from the window. Fromm had positioned his desk—strewn with books and manuscripts—in front of the picture window that extended across the room so that his gaze always fell on the water and its dramatic interplay with light. On the opposite shore, the peak of Mt. Gambarogno was visible through the sunny haze of the late summer afternoon.

Not until later did I become aware to what degree a person's relationship with nature instinctively creates a sense of trust in me. Here, I had apparently encountered another human being who shared my affinity. Fromm offered me a chair next to this desk, facing the room. The bookshelves were overflowing, with manuscripts, handwritten drafts, and notes piled on every conceivable surface. This rather chaotic environment became obscured, however, when he seated himself and focused on me with an indescribable expression in his eyes.

Face to face

Fromm looked at me in such a straightforward way that my attempts at polite conversation ceased abruptly and any superficial courtesies became unnecessary. Although we had only met face-to-face a few moments before, a dimension for the relationship had already emerged, one that allowed for closeness and trust, but no longer allowed for the evasion of a question or topic with clever remarks. Somehow Fromm's eyes, encircled by wrinkles and scrutinizing me intently, managed to initiate a conversation that allayed my anxieties and made it possible for me to concentrate intently.

The initial focus of our meeting was by no means my questions about his work and thought. Fromm inquired about my professional situation and why I was interested in his ideas, particularly his ethics. Above all, he asked which aspects of psychoanalysis, religion, and theology interested me. He even wanted to know my stance on Germany's *Ostpolitik*, my opinion of the Bavarian-born politician Franz Josef Strauss, and my assessment of Konrad Lorenz's theory of aggression. It wasn't his intention, however, to discern my political or ideological orientation as quickly as possible. The questions—as it became clear to me through our conversations over the following eight years—were intended to reveal my deepest concerns and preoccupations. Fromm wanted to understand my innermost being: if and what I loved and hated, valued and sought, critically assessed and rejected, what appealed to me, encouraged, stimulated, and angered me, delighted or thrilled me, what made me feel anxious or guilty, or what frightened me. He was curious about my feelings, my needs, my interests, and my passions.

This was something entirely new to me. It was not my "head," my thoughts, my intellectual abilities, or my sophistication that interested him, but—to continue on the same metaphorical level—my "heart." What motivated me, fascinated me, passionately moved me, what was behind my values and compelled me—this is what he wanted to learn. Thinking, the art of argument, brainwork, knowledge—all of these were at most means for arriving at what really drove people.

Much later I came to realize that the therapeutic focus of the psychoanalysis I had undergone over the course of my university education could be valid for every human encounter, and that Fromm actually advocated a way of life with goals different from those familiar to me from the academic world of the humanities. There, the mind, the faculty of memory, the capacity for conceptual and intellectual thinking were trained in order to gain control over the will, affects, and needs. This was reputedly the only way to communicate and to conduct scholarship: without the distracting interference of feelings.

In contrast, Fromm's undivided attention was directed toward coming into contact with inner strivings and feelings, understanding them not as obstructing but as bearing energy. Even if the emotional energies were less than flattering, preventing thinking and acting in line with reality, it was crucial to make contact with them and meet them with understanding. Only in this way could the hidden meaning of intense feelings, such as jealousy or a paralyzing sense of inferiority, for example, be recognized, and the energy bound there be released for a rational or loving approach. The result was a school of thought in which "head" and "heart" were linked and that strove for cognitive insights *based on feelings*. Consequently, it comes as no surprise that Fromm placed particular emphasis on the fundamental role of feelings.

Through his interest and questions, Fromm wanted to get in touch with my inner world, my rational and irrational, overt and covert strivings. To do so, he used eye contact. Since infancy we have all learned to express our inner state—our affects, feelings, wishes, and needs, as well as our inner reactions—through eye contact.

Naturally, at the time, I was incapable of fully comprehending this. What I did sense, however, was that Fromm had a special way of approaching me: it had a great deal to do with his gaze, which one could hardly evade. The pupils of his blue, myopic eyes behind the rimless eyeglasses appeared to be diminished in size, causing his look to seem almost penetrating. His gaze corresponded to his way of being interested in my inner life, my soul.

But there was something else about the way Fromm looked at me, spoke to me, and focused the conversation. Despite the directness and bluntness with which he approached the uncovering of my soul, I did not at all feel interrogated, cornered, judged, unmasked, or exposed. I quickly sensed that he was dealing with me in a pleasant way, with understanding and warm-heartedness, and that I had no inclination to justify or conceal myself. He reached out to me and, through his sincere interest in what concerned me, let me sense that there was no reason to fear for myself or my inner world. Every look and every word conveyed a sense of solidarity and kindness.

This type of human encounter was an entirely new experience for me: this way of conversing, of being with the other, of venturing into that world of feelings and passions at work behind our thinking. With the reassurance of a well-meaning glance from the other person, small talk or pretenses become unnecessary. Initiated by Fromm, this experience signaled the beginning of a new intellectual approach for me.

Letting someone sense: "This is you"

The Frommian art of living has its roots in Fromm's own experiences of therapeutic relationships. Approximately twenty years later, as his literary executor, I was preparing a number of Fromm's unpublished manuscripts for publication, when I came across the transcript of a lecture he had held at the William Alanson White Institute in New York City in 1959. Here he describes this precise experience of solidarity:

> The feeling of human solidarity is one of the most important therapeutic experiences which we can give to the patient, because at that moment the patient does not feel isolated any more. In all his neuroses or whatever his troubles are, the feeling of isolation, whether he is aware of it or not, is the very crux of his suffering. There are many other cruxes, but this is the main one. At the moment when he senses that I share this with him, so that I can say, "This is you," and I can say it not kindly and not unkindly, this is a tremendous relief from isolation. Another person who says, "This is you," and stays with me, and shares this with me.
>
> I have had the experience increasingly through the years that once you speak from your own experience and in this kind of relatedness to the patient, you can say anything and the patient will not feel hurt. On the contrary, he will feel greatly relieved that there is one man who sees him, because he knows the story all the time. We are often so naive to think the patient must not know this, and the patient must not know that, because he would be so shocked. The fact is the patient knows it all the time, except he does not permit himself to have this knowledge consciously. When we say it, he is relieved because he can say: "For heaven's sake, I knew this always."
>
> *Dealing with the Unconscious in Psychotherapeutic Practice,*
> 1992g [1959], pp. 107–108

What Fromm said here about the therapeutic relationship also held true for him in general. In every type of relationship, there should be a direct meeting with the other person, a face-to-face encounter; the face reveals the inner world of the other. A face-to-face encounter goes beneath the surface, making a "central relatedness" possible:

> I can explain the other person as another Ego, as another thing, and then look at him as I look at my car, my house, my neurosis, whatever it may be. Or I can relate to this other person in the sense of being him, in the sense of experiencing, feeling this other person. Then I do not think about myself, then my Ego does not stand in my way. But something entirely different happens. There is what I call a *central relatedness* between me and him. He is not a thing over there which I look at, but he confronts me fully and I confront him fully, and there in fact is no way of escape.
>
> pp. 97–98

Such a direct encounter means to be interested:

> We are interested in another person, we listen attentively, we listen with interest, we think about the person, and yet the other person remains outside (. . .). We should try to be aware of the difference between lack of interest, interest and what I call *the direct meeting with the other person*, not only with regard to our patients, but with regard to everybody.
>
> p. 105; italics added

What distinguishes this "direct" meeting with another person from "interest" in another person? The direct meeting facilitates coming into contact with the feelings and passions of the other in order to be able to experience him or her as a whole person. For Fromm, there is one definitive characteristic of this kind of direct encounter with someone else: "If you really see a person (. . .) you will stop judging provided you see that person fully" (p. 106). No matter how often we are forced to pass judgment on what we want and what we resist in the course of living and safeguarding our existence, in a direct meeting, in a direct encounter with the other, we must refrain from judgment, if we truly want to see him or her. "If you see yourself, whatever you are, you will stop feeling guilty, because you feel: 'This is me.'"

Significant in both the meeting and the encounter is their directness:

> At the moment when you see yourself or another person fully, you do not judge because you are overwhelmed with the feeling, with the experience: "So this is you," and also with the experience: "And who am I to judge?" In fact, you do not even ask that question. Because in experiencing him, you experience yourself. You say: "So that is you" and you feel in some way very plainly: "And that is me too." (...) If I see the other person—what happens is not only that I stop judging but also that I have a sense of union, of sharing, of oneness, which is something much stronger than being kind or being nice. There is a feeling of human solidarity when two people—or even one person—can say to the other: "So that is you, and I share this with you." This is a tremendously important experience. I would say, short of complete love, it is the most gratifying, the most wonderful, the most exhilarating experience, which occurs between two people.

p. 107

An exhilarating experience

I began to perceive Fromm's capability for the face-to-face encounter when I met him for the first time personally on this first day of September in Locarno. Exactly thirty-three years earlier, the Second World War had begun with the invasion of Poland. Jewish by birth, Fromm was able to avoid persecution and genocide by emigrating to the USA in 1934. Sadly, although he had done everything in his power from New York City to arrange for the emigration of relatives, for whom he cared deeply, he was only able save a few from deportation to concentration camps and their subsequent murder.

Auschwitz, however, did not deter Fromm from seeking the face-to-face encounter with the other. Nor did he need transcendental authorization or a justification beyond man in order to have "the most exhilarating experience which occurs between two people." The practice or use of the capacity for the direct encounter requires neither rational proof nor special justification. In the course of its realization it proves itself to be morally right and good. The only question is what prevents one from actually encountering the other—the capability to encounter oneself and others directly can be limited, neutralized, or even thwarted by fears, prejudices, biases, illusions, inhibitions, fixations, etc. To put it concisely, for Fromm it wasn't the head that makes decisions but the heart, through emotional and psychic drives. These drives determine to a great degree whether or not our thinking is rational and reality-based, and whether or not our feeling embodies love and solidarity. This is why Fromm generally spoke of the capacity for reason and love instead of for the direct meeting. The practice of reason and love is what ultimately makes exhilarating experiences possible.

During our first personal encounter I had the impression that the arguments with which I had intended to dispute Fromm's humanism were now obtuse and beside the point. With my intellectual weapons, that is, logical arguments, I had wanted to challenge, not concede, I had wanted to be right, not rational. While I had sought confrontation, Fromm offered a face-to-face encounter. The way he approached me was completely disarming.

I accepted his offer and noticed how our two encounters during my initial visit invigorated me. I left Locarno highly motivated and energized. In the following weeks, I formulated the sections on Fromm's social psychology and his theory of character orientation for my dissertation, and visited him in Locarno again in the summer of 1973. The next summer Fromm—who until then had only spent the summer months in Switzerland and otherwise lived in Cuernavaca, Mexico— decided not to return to Mexico, but to reside in Locarno year-round. This is how he came to ask me to be his research assistant, while he was writing the book *To Have Or to Be?* (1976a). I lived in Locarno for some time and later I worked for him while based in Tübingen, visiting him regularly in Locarno as well as in Hinterzarten and Baden-Baden, two spas in the Black Forest where he and Annis spent the hot summer days together.

Above all, the almost daily contact with Fromm in 1974 and 1975 gave me the opportunity to develop an understanding of his art of living by observing and reflecting on its effects. When our discussions turned to the practice of reason and love, and to the "productive orientation" of man's impulses, this exemplified life as an art. Actually, Fromm spoke of the "art of living," as well as the "art of life," long before the philosophy of the art of life, the "ars vivendi," was rediscovered (see for example *The Art of Being*, 1989a [1974–75]).

Our conversations revolved in part around topics that I had researched for *To Have Or to Be?*, for example, the concept of activity in Aristotle, or studies on the oral tradition of the Sermon on the Mount in the New Testament or the concept of the Godhead in Meister Eckhart. The other part of the conversations—usually continuing for three or four hours—focused on specific passages and chapters of the book in progress, which Fromm had given me to read as soon as Joan Hughes, his British secretary, had typed the handwritten version from yellow legal pads. What distinctly characterized these conversations were Fromm's elucidations based on his vast reservoir of historical and political knowledge as well as his personal experiences and encounters with important figures in politics, society, and psychoanalysis. Equally unforgettable: his boundless trove of jokes from the Jewish and psychoanalytic scenes. It was extraordinarily difficult for Fromm to refrain from telling a joke if one suddenly came to mind.

But it wasn't actually the topics under discussion that caused me to notice the effects of his art of living, as interesting and entertaining as these were. It was the face-to-face encounter that Fromm made possible, regardless of the subject matter, which had clearly perceptible effects on me. Particularly conspicuous were my heightened attentiveness and ability to concentrate; our interpersonal communication did not consume strength but released energy instead. During our countless discussions, I never experienced a feeling of exhaustion or a decline in attentiveness. I was wide awake and on some evenings worked on my dissertation far into the night after our meeting, the hours spent together with Fromm having been energizing and stimulating. Equally striking was that I often lost all sense of time. Often it seemed as if I had arrived half an hour earlier, although three or four hours had actually elapsed.

Only in retrospect did the impact of these encounters with Fromm become clear to me; his contact with my emotional realm and my own driving forces had apparently initiated a process of personal growth, although in all those years I never experienced Fromm in a therapeutic setting. (Since, according to Fromm, the most significant therapeutic factor is the capacity of the therapist for a *direct meeting*—a face-to-face encounter with the patient—and not a setting defined as "therapy," it is not surprising that I observed typical therapeutic effects outside the therapeutic setting.) Nor did we ever discuss the following observations.

As a result of my contact with Fromm, I began to sense and seek a relationship with nature again. During childhood I had always known whether the moon was full, or waxing or waning, or new at a particular moment. Now I had rediscovered the lunar phases and was captivated when the full moon was reflected in the lake, illuminating the snow-covered peaks. On January 4, 1975, the first red bud of the camellia in front of my window in the Via Mondacce burst into bloom, and before long there was no mountain peak on the horizon that I hadn't scaled.

My decision to stop smoking in the spring of 1975 made life exceedingly difficult for me. Over an extended period of time, cigarettes had supported and stabilized something within me. I was oriented toward "having" the cigarettes and toward the nicotine-related effects of smoking. But who was I without the cigarettes? As a nonsmoker? The intense daily work on the manuscripts of *To Have Or to Be?* was not without consequence. Freeing myself from this having mode of existence became a moment of truth: would I only discuss the choice of having vs. being intelligently, or would I dare to put theory to practice, i.e., dare to try to *be* without the crutch of *having*? The withdrawal symptoms were intense, and it took me several months to realize consciously and fully that the alternative to the having mode of existence is *not* not-having, but being. Being, as I learned, had much to do with becoming aware of other things in oneself and in one's social context as well as with allowing and pursuing new interests.

This was *terra incognita* for me, on which I trod with a wish for professional reorientation. I wanted to discover—in a more exacting and professional way—what really motivated and drove me as well as others; I wanted to familiarize myself with approaches to the human unconscious. At the same time, I became aware that what interested me and what sparked my interest in scholarly work was changing considerably. To determine and justify what is morally right, morally demanded, and morally favorable, in other words, the morally good, is undeniably important and challenging. However, it became increasingly clear to me that another question preoccupied me much more, namely, why do people who recognize the morally right and good not act in accordance with these insights. What hinders them from using their powers of reason? What irrational forces lead to their failure to act rationally? I wanted to undergo training in psychoanalysis and leave the fields of theology and ethics, which I consequently did in 1977, after completing a doctoral dissertation on Fromm's ethics (see Funk, 1978) and having been accepted into a psychoanalytic training program in Stuttgart.

It wasn't only the change in career direction, however, that allowed me to sense the effects of Fromm's insights on me. I had also met the woman whom I would later marry, and had sensed the wish, nurtured by Eros and a love for life, to share and sustain life. What an awakening it is to experience personally how life and the potential for growth take shape in one's own children!

Encountering the stranger

Every direct encounter with the self, every face-to-face encounter with other people that is actually realized, constitutes an advance in the art of living. The art is not a school of thought, not a compendium of behavior, not a list of steps for developing social competence, neither expertise nor a therapeutic technique to be implemented, and not a think tank for *la bella vita*. It is a form of the direct or face-to-face encounter—with one's own self in the stranger and the stranger in one's self. This kind of living changes those who practice it.

How crucial the direct encounter with the self is and what consequences it can have were phenomena that I initially observed with Fromm himself. Hardly a day went by when he did not actively seek this direct encounter with himself. Fromm usually allotted an hour in the late morning for his exercises. What he meant were physical and contemplative exercises that he had described in *The Art of Being* (1989a [1974–75]). Promoting mindfulness and self-awareness, they included sensory awareness exercises, Tai Chi, as well as self-analysis. He concentrated on his body movements and on his breathing, attempting to become totally empty and meditate. He also tried to become aware of what resounded in him emotionally or preoccupied him mentally: for example, a feeling of unease that persisted after an interview, or the impulse to write a letter to the editor of the *New York Times*. Whenever he could remember a dream from the night before, he tried to decipher its message in order to be able to confront his own unconscious strivings, fantasies, emotions, and conflicts.

The effects of these exercises that sought the direct encounter with the self were apparent, not only to Fromm himself but to those around him as well. The most impressive example for me was the opening address Fromm gave at a symposium in Locarno-Muralto in May 1975. Together with the Gottlieb Duttweiler Institute in Switzerland, I had organized this symposium in honor of Fromm's seventy-fifth birthday. During the preceding weeks, Fromm had been considerably incapacitated by a broken arm, and for a long time it had been uncertain whether he would be able to deliver the opening address. He ultimately spoke extemporaneously for two hours on *The Relevance of Psychoanalysis for the Future* (1992h [1975]). Afterward I asked him where he had found the concentration and energy for the lecture, and he replied, without any pretense whatsoever: "Well, this morning I spent twice as long doing my exercises."

Someone who practices the direct encounter with himself can draw on powers that serve the direct encounter with other people, facilitating total absorption in a topic and in the other person. The opposite is also true: Someone who practices the direct encounter with others draws on experiences that facilitate the encounter with the stranger without and within.

That Fromm was versed in both, and consequently able to be with himself and the other, could readily be seen in his facial expression. After his death, I found a series of photographs of Fromm, taken with the assistance of a photographic innovation (a battery-powered rewinding mechanism) that allowed an entire series of photographs to be shot within a few seconds. On the strip of developed negatives, one photograph showed Fromm with his eyes shut next to another photograph in which he was looking directly at the photographer. In the course of these sequential images, Fromm must have closed his eyes for a split second and been photographed in the process. On closer scrutiny this photograph depicts a face concentrated on the inner self, a face totally immersed within. The adjacent photograph of Fromm with his eyes wide open gives the impression that his eyes focus on the observer. In the first, he is totally with himself, in the second, he is totally with the other.

These portraits reveal how intensely Fromm must have practiced the direct encounter so as to learn to be with himself and with another. At the same time, they illustrate the significance of the practice of the direct encounter for the successful realization of humanity and of society. Regardless of the type of relationship in which the direct or face-to-face encounter is carried out, in relationship to others, in scholarly or scientific work, in artistic or therapeutic endeavors, in connection with nature, or in connection with one's own inner powers, the direct encounter always releases energy for direct encounters in other areas of life.

The experience drawn from the practice of the face-to-face encounter inspired Fromm's development of the concepts of "productive character orientation," "biophilia," and the "being mode of existence." "The person who fully lives life is attracted by the process of life and growth in all spheres," writes Fromm in *The Heart of Man* (1964a, p. 47). In *To Have Or to Be?* (1976a) he summarizes the exponential effect of the direct encounter as follows: "Genuine love increases the capacity to love and to give to others. The true lover loves the whole world, in his or her love for a specific person" (p. 107). In the having mode of existence, every instance of sharing and every use of what one has leads to its consumption and its consequent loss. Sharing and using by a person in the being mode of existence lead to the experience of abundance and to the growth of the individual's own powers in their very use.

Whenever I wanted to comprehend more fully what Fromm actually meant by "productivity," "reason and love as [one's] own powers," "biophilia," or the "being mode of existence," I found it helpful to recall the effects of the face-to-face encounters with him.

Fromm's capacity for the face-to-face encounter ultimately explains why his writings have a special appeal for many people, particularly those who have difficulty reading and comprehending highly conceptual, abstract theories. In an interview conducted by Hans Jürgen Schultz (*In the Name of Life. A Portrait through Dialogue?* [1974b]), Fromm confessed: "I have no gift for abstract thought. I can think only those thoughts that relate to something I can concretely experience" (p. 105). This is why Fromm also sought a direct encounter with any issue or problem under consideration in his written work. Before beginning to write, he had to find a mental but not unemotional approach to what others had written on the same question. When reading a primary text, it was vital that he could directly relate to what he was reading. With certain authors this was regularly the case—above all Sigmund Freud and Karl Marx, Baruch Spinoza and Meister Eckhart. With a number of other authors this was rarely so—for example, Georg Wilhelm Hegel, Martin Heidegger, Theodor W. Adorno, and most sociologists.

Fromm spent much more time reading than writing (perhaps twenty or thirty times as much). When he finally did start to write, he generally put his ideas on that specific topic on paper in one sitting—by hand, preferably with a fountain pen or ballpoint pen. The following day he read what he had written the day before and sometimes started over from the beginning if he had been unable to express what concerned and interested him, and what he wanted to say. He would make another attempt until he felt that he had become one with the topic. While writing, Fromm also sought the direct encounter, namely, with a topic, with concepts, arguments, and ideas; not until he was convinced that this encounter had been correctly conveyed in the written text did he give the handwritten text to his secretary, so that she could prepare a typewritten manuscript, which he could then give others to read.

Because Fromm's writings arose out of a direct and inner encounter with the works of other writers and with a topic, and were not the outgrowth of abstract thought and logical thought processes, many readers feel addressed by them and are able to enter into an inner dialogue with what they read. This once again shows that Fromm neither wanted nor founded a school of thought. Fromm lived and felt what he said and wrote. His own art of living sets an example.

Of course, this example does not require textbooks and therapy manuals. Fromm's teachings and life are intertwined with his person and writings because both relate to the achievement of direct encounters. But what conditions does his art of living require in order to teach us something? And how might it ultimately be learned?

The art of living as direct encounter

Fromm's art of living is, as already indicated, an *art of direct, felt encounter with oneself in the stranger and the stranger in oneself.*

> This attitude toward the "stranger" is inseparable from the attitude toward oneself. As long as any fellow being is experienced as fundamentally different from myself, as long as he remains a stranger, I remain a stranger to myself too. When I experience myself fully, then I recognize that I am the same as any other human being, that I am the child, the sinner, the saint, the one who hopes and the one who despairs, the one who can feel joy and the one who can feel sadness. I discover that only the thought concepts, the customs, the surface are different, and that the human substance is the same. I discover that I am everybody, and that I discover myself in discovering my fellow man, and vice versa. In this experience I discover what humanity is, I discover the One Man.
>
> *Beyond the Chains of Illusion*, 1962a, p. 171

How can one learn to discover oneself in a stranger? And how does an encounter with the stranger in oneself happen? But, above all, how can the art of living be realized not only as a theory and body of knowledge, relegated to the realm of good intentions, but above all as something that determines the practice of thought, feeling, and action? The art of living enables a *direct* encounter, an actual, unmediated sense and experience of the stranger in oneself and an unmediated feeling of oneself in the stranger.

It is this qualification of directness that makes the art of living so challenging and difficult. Direct means *free of* hindrances, such as preconceived notions, fantasies, concepts, prejudices, irrational feelings, strivings, and passions, and *free for* an immediately perceived, desired, and felt encounter. Most important, direct means an encounter with feelings and passions, our own and others'. This very demand already poses a challenge for many because feelings and passions are often not experienced as animating forces but rather as sand in the gears.

Such a direct encounter becomes even more difficult when we assume that strong emotional forces determine our thought, feelings, and actions without our conscious awareness. How can we be capable of a direct encounter if we have no awareness of the unconscious forces within ourselves and others?

The Frommian art of living is indeed demanding. Neither easy nor learned without effort, it always requires that we become *free of* something so that we can be *free for* something. One must let go in order to realize that one has become and now is free for something. Most important, the art requires that we recognize the degree to which we and others are moved by emotions of which we are not conscious. Fromm's art of living therefore relies on the insights of Freud about roads to the unconscious. This is the focus of the first chapter. Moreover, Fromm sees the individual as decisively shaped by social forces. I discuss this in the second chapter, which explains Fromm's sociopsychological approach.

The conditions that would enable us to ask what allows mankind to thrive are only created when we are able to see that our thoughts, feelings, and actions are dependent upon unconscious *and* social forces.

This is focus of the third chapter. Precisely because every person is always already a social being, the success of the individual requires that he use his psychological powers to contribute to the success of society. To be sure, social coexistence can also lead to the development of psychological strivings that hinder or even thwart human well-being. In the fourth chapter, four examples show how social well-being can take place at the expense of human well-being and what the individual should do to privilege human flourishing.

This preview already makes clear that the art of living according to Fromm is not a guide to behavior and not a manual, nor is it a set of instructions that one simply needs to apply. The following chapters speak solely to the preconditions required for living in this specific way. This also holds for the closing fifth chapter, which deals with ways toward direct encounter and introduces those preparatory exercises and practices that Fromm himself did every day.

"Learning" does not take place through the accumulation of knowledge and intellectual control, but rather through a certain practice of living, that is, the felt and experienced direct encounter with oneself, with a stranger, or with an idea. For that reason, the art of living outlined here describes only those requirements and paths *toward* direct encounter. The paths *of* direct encounter can only be walked by each individual alone.

Even though the Frommian art of living indicates that each individual's life process is the place of learning, the question remains: How did Fromm himself "learn" the prerequisites for direct encounter that the chapters discuss? In answer, each chapter begins with a biographical context that illustrates his learning about these aspects of the art of living.

The first and perhaps most important step that Fromm took in his life of learning was to discover the meaning of the unconscious and track roads to it, much in the manner that Freud did in creating psychoanalysis.

Figure 2 Fromm as a student, 1920. © Lit Fromm Estate.

Roads to the Unconscious

Fromm's road to psychoanalysis

Five days before his death on March 18, 1980, Fromm gave an interview to Guido Ferrari of Ticino television. Ferrari asked Fromm about the most important events in his life. Fromm named the First World War as a decisive experience for him. At that time, he was concerned with the question of how

> people who don't know each other and have nothing against each other, can kill each other, can allow themselves to be killed. Who is behind this? Who profits from this? What sort of meaning does this have?
>
> This question of World War I: "How is it possible?" was probably the most important motivation for my thinking as a youth, from age 16 on. And ever since it has remained the main motivation behind my thought: how is it possible that people in masses can behave so irrationally and be so easily seduced? And of course, too: what can people do to diminish the seduction?
>
> *Mut zum Sein*, 1980e

Fromm himself published practically nothing autobiographical. Only a brief chapter, "Some Personal Antecedents," which introduces his book *Beyond the Chains of Illusion* (1962a, pp. 3–12), offers a little information about how Fromm, at the start of the 1920s, was tormented by questions to which Freud and psychoanalysis ultimately provided some answers. In this chapter, he recalls an attractive painter acquainted with his family. She was so attached to her widowed father that she twice broke her engagement with her fiancé in order to live together with her father. When her father died, the young woman took her own life and requested in her will that she be buried together with him. Fromm remarks how deeply the suicide of this woman for whom he cared both haunted and puzzled him. Only ten years later, with the help of Freud's psychoanalysis, did he find an answer.

Whether it be the hatred and mass killing of war or a woman who kills herself because of an incestuous parent–child fixation, irrational forces had to be at work in both cases, determining human behavior despite all better judgment. Fromm admits: "I was deeply troubled by questions with regard to individual and social phenomena, and I was eager for an answer" (*Beyond the Chains of Illusion*, 1962a, p. 9).

Fromm's introduction to Freudian psychoanalysis at the start of the 1920s was not accidental:

> If I want to understand how the problem of why people act the way they do became of such paramount interest to me, it might be sufficient to assume that having been an only child, with an anxious and moody father and a depression-prone mother, was enough to arouse my interest in the strange and mysterious reasons for human reactions.
>
> *Beyond the Chains of Illusion*, 1962a, pp. 3–4

In answer to Ferrari's question of how he came to psychoanalysis, Fromm replied: "because I myself was a pretty neurotic young person like most of us who become psychoanalysts" (*Mut zum Sein*, 1980e).

And yet, Fromm's actual path to psychoanalysis would be a different one. His girlfriend, and later wife, Frieda Reichmann introduced him to Freudian psychoanalysis, in theoretical and practical terms. With regard to theory, Reichmann had completed her psychoanalytic training with Hanns Sachs in Berlin and worked as a psychiatrist in a sanatorium in the Weisser Hirsch district of Dresden. She shared her enthusiasm with her then boyfriend Erich, eleven years her junior, about the unimagined possibilities of liberating people from their fears, compulsions, and inhibitions by helping them to become conscious of their repressed sexual impulses.

Fromm came to know psychoanalysis from a more practical perspective when, in 1924, they opened a "Thorapeutikum" together at 15 Moenchhof Street in Heidelberg, in which a generally Jewish clientele was analyzed on the couch by Frieda Reichmann. Erich Fromm, too, was on the couch in analysis with Frieda Reichmann. Fromm's first psychoanalysis, however, ended because Fromm had fallen in love with Reichmann—they married in 1926. A second analysis, with Wilhelm Wittenberg in Munich, followed, and Fromm's analysis with Hanns Sachs in Berlin, which took place within his training to become a psychoanalyst, ended in 1930. (For biographical details, see among others Funk, 1983, 2000; 2006; Schröter, 2015.)

There is no indication that Fromm came to psychoanalysis because of any concrete psychic distress, although his less than happy marriage with Reichmann and the pressure his parents put on him were no doubt distressing. More likely, Fromm was captivated by a profound interest in human behavior. Already in his teenage studies of the Talmud as well as later as a university student, he sought to determine the right path within the Jewish religious tradition. In light of the many contradictions within human behavior, Fromm wanted to know about those forces not subject to reason that influence human behavior.

We can most clearly see how therapeutic processes put pressure on Fromm and led to fundamental life shifts by looking at his changed attitude toward the religion of his forefathers.

Raised in an Orthodox Jewish home, he was nicknamed "pious" by his fellow students. (The German word for "pious" is "fromm." The students would taunt: "Make me as fromm as Fromm, so that into heaven I may come!") Fromm originally wanted to become a Talmudic scholar. To do so, he would have needed to leave his parents, something he dared not do because of his father. In a 1979 interview with Gérard Khoury, Fromm explained:

> What I wanted to do was actually to go to one of the Talmudic Universities in Lithuania. It was my great wish to become a Talmudic scholar but that evoked such a fierce reaction on my father's side that I couldn't do it without hurting him so deeply, that I had not the courage or maybe the wish to do so. Thus I gave up this project—I would say today fortunately—to become a Talmudic scholar.
>
> *Interview*, 2000f [1979]

Instead, Fromm studied law for two semesters in his hometown of Frankfurt starting in 1918, before moving to Heidelberg in 1919, where he shifted his studies to economics and sociology.

It seems likely that Fromm's relationship with his father and the related question of religion stood at the center of his psychoanalyses. Together with Reichmann, on the Jewish holiday of Passover in 1926 Fromm waged his first "attack" on his father as an attack on religion. They did what is taboo for any Jew, especially in light of their "Thorapeutikum," which strictly followed Jewish dietary laws. Reichmann (1954) writes in her memoirs: "So Passover, Erich and I went into a park in Heidelberg and ate (leavened) bread. We couldn't do it at home because there were these people, who after all relied on us." The meaning that eating the leavened bread actually had that day is explained by a sentence Fromm wrote forty years later:

> Passover is the celebration of the liberation from slavery, and as the *Haggadah* says, every person must feel as if he himself had been a slave in Egypt and had been liberated from there. The *matzot,* or unleavened bread, which is eaten during the week of Passover, is a symbol of wandering.
>
> *You Shall Be as Gods,* 1966a, pp. 71–72

This "fall from grace" was an act of liberation for Fromm. He freed himself forever from the religion of his fathers.

The subject of his father, however, did not end there, as we see in Fromm's conflict with his training analyst Hanns Sachs, with whom he did his final analysis from 1928 to 1930. In Fromm's eyes, Sachs's face was less than attractive. With barely any chin, Sachs struck Fromm as having the face of a pig. Gérard Khoury documented this attack on the therapy-father in his recorded interview of 1979 (which Fromm had described to me in the same words):

> With Doctor Sachs I did one of the more courageous things. (...) Since I was a very conscientious pupil, knowing one has to say everything, even if it was very difficult, I thought I had better start out with this;

then there is nothing worse that can come, and so I said, looking at Doctor Sachs: "Since I have to say everything, I want to tell you that when I saw you the first time I thought you have a face like a pig."

Interview, 2000f [1979]

Clearly there was no beating about the bush in Fromm's analysis with Sachs. In his transference onto the analyst, Fromm presented for treatment his problem with his father. Although Fromm already knew everything about the possibility of repression, his attack shows an unconscious, because repressed, hostility toward his father with which the 28-year old still struggled.

The unconscious as repressed

Freud, confessed Fromm shortly before his death, "opened a new world for me, namely the world of the unconscious (...) in the sense of the repressed" (1980e). Freud primarily saw in the unconscious those feelings, wishes, ideas, impulses, and perceptions that are repressed because they are experienced as unpleasant, either scorned by society or in conflict with one's own values. They are prevented from penetrating into consciousness by other forces or by false justifications (rationalizations).

Fromm names as an example:

a father with sadistic impulses, who tends to punish and mistreat his children. But he is convinced that he beats them because that is the only way to teach them virtue and to protect them from doing evil. He is not aware of any sadistic satisfaction—he is only aware of the rationalization, his idea of duty and of the right method of bringing up children.

Beyond the Chains of Illusion, 1962a, p. 90

The purpose of repression is always to prevent oneself from perceiving certain feelings and passions, ideas and impulses, and with this rationalization thereby to construct another sort of truth about what drives and motivates us, and then to defend this conscious motive.

> If anyone would tell [the sadistic father] the truth, that is to say, mention to him that behind his sanctimonious rationalizations are the very desires which he bitterly disapproves of, he would sincerely feel indignant or misunderstood and falsely accused. This passionate refusal to admit the existence of what is repressed, Freud called "resistance." Its strength is roughly in proportion to the strength of the repressive tendencies.
>
> *Beyond the Chains of Illusion*, 1962a, pp. 90–91

It sounds paradoxical: precisely this stubborn resistance is often the best indication that the truth and actual awareness must not come to light. If the rationalization were wrongly called into question and the person falsely accused of repression, then he would be able to react calmly and not bark like a dog that's been hit. In the case of actual resistance, the reaction would be accompanied by irritation, anger, and aggression.

> When people hear what they do not want to hear, they become angry. They want, as it were, to wipe out the witness to their crimes. They can't very well kill him—that's a bit too risky—so they dispose of him in a symbolic way. They blow up and say, "You're speaking out of jealousy, out of some base motive. You hate me. You get pleasure out of saying nasty things about me."
>
> *Psychology for Nonpsychologists*, 1974a, p. 76

Let us return once again to the example of the sadistic father. Suppose he does not respond with resistance, but rather is capable of understanding that his use of these educational measures inflicts pain on the other. Then he begins to question his own rationalization, and the sadistic impulse is no longer repressed. But it also does not vanish into thin air. Instead, the impulse is no longer acted out, which at least protects his children from further harm. The question remains as to whether the sadistic impulse will seek another outlet. For example, perhaps instead of beating his children the father treats them with contempt, or humiliates them, or he finds another victim for his sadism. Possible defenses associated with the sadistic impulse will be discussed in more detail later.

To stay with this example, the only real solution would be if the father could come to understand what motivates him to treat his children in such a sadistic manner. Perhaps he could recall how powerless *he* felt as a child when he was beaten by his own father. And perhaps in his powerless rage, he swore revenge that once he grew up and had power over others, he would let them know this feeling. He would have to relive his own pain and powerless rage in order to understand that he still cannot forget these feelings and for that reason revisits them on his children. Only then would the father become emotionally conscious of the unconscious forces behind his sadism, and only then would the sadistic impulses lose their source of sustenance. The repetition compulsion, which continually causes the father to re-experience his unbearable feeling of impotence in vengeful ways, could finally end.

The example of repressed sadistic impulses fed by an unconscious, powerless rage illustrates how we can gain access to the unconscious by accepting the existence of repressed perceptions, feelings, and aspirations. Further paths to the unconscious will be discussed after we have explored the ways in which Freud's recognition of repression and of the rationalization of repressed passions shattered any faith in reason and in conscious thought.

The power of rationalization

For Fromm, it was Freud who

saw how unreal most of what we think about ourselves is, how we deceive ourselves continuously about ourselves and about others; he was prompted by the passionate interest to touch the reality, which is behind our conscious thought. Freud recognized that *most of what is real within ourselves is not conscious, and that most of what is conscious is not real.* This devotion to the search for inner reality opened up a new dimension of truth.

Beyond the Chains of Illusion, 1962a, p. 89

One of the primary things that psychoanalytic thinking does is to put into question all that is customary.

If our conscious thinking is not a reliable starting point, which thoughts, ideas, and arguments remain valid and true?

> Before Freud, it was generally believed that unless a person were lying his conscious thoughts are what he *really* thinks. Freud discovered that a person can be fully sincere, subjectively, and yet that his thought may have little weight or reality.
>
> *May Man Prevail*, 1961a, p. 127

When we use rationalizations, we have no sense that we are lying. We do not realize that we have succumbed to a deception in our thinking and arguments. And this is usually all the more the case when we muster all our strength and reason to make our thoughts true and convincing.

We cannot recognize and unmask a rationalization as such if we judge it only by its logical consistency and the power of its argument. *What* someone thinks is not decisive, but rather *how* he thinks, because this can show the function that thinking has and if the actual goal of the thinking is to legitimize a certain behavior. In that case, argument is tasked with justifying a passion that is acceptable neither to oneself nor to others. For that reason, psychoanalysis posits "that only by understanding the unconscious processes going on in [someone] can we know whether he rationalizes or whether he speaks the truth" (*Psychoanalysis and Religion*, 1950a, p. 60).

Fromm formulates this even more pointedly in his later work:

> Since Freud also the moral problem is to be reconsidered: A person is responsible not only for what he thinks but for his own unconscious. This is where responsibility begins, the rest is mask, the rest is nothing; what a person believes is hardly worth listening to.
>
> *Therapeutic Aspects of Psychoanalysis*, 1991d [1974], p. 74

Psychoanalysis relativizes the human capacity for reason while simultaneously relying on its illuminating power. "Psychoanalysis while debunking rationalizations has made reason the tool with which we achieve such critical analyses of rationalization" (*Psychoanalysis and Religion*, 1950a, p. 57).

> To help man discern truth from falsehood in himself is the basic aim of psychoanalysis, a therapeutic method which is an empirical application of the statement, "The truth shall make you free."
>
> [Jn 8:32] pp. 77–78

Fromm never tired of emphasizing the question of truth behind all rationalizations and illusions of thought as the main concern for Freud as well as himself, and thereby, despite all skepticism about conscious thought, continued to rely on a capacity for critical reason. The critical nature of reason means nothing other than exploring conscious and unconscious emotional forces as well as the rational or irrational dynamics that inform them. Someone who says he has the best in mind for his child and professes this verbosely may have eyes that betray a different, more loveless story. Words may be an attempt to cover what the eyes reveal.

Indicators of the unconscious

We have seen how Fromm's personal journey to psychoanalysis and working with the unconscious came about, as well as the meaning repression had for Freud as a road to the unconscious. Since there are many unconscious barriers that prevent a directly felt encounter with ourselves and with others, it will be helpful to get to know other signs of the unconscious in our introduction to Fromm's art of living. (Self-)deception and false justifications in the form of *rationalizations* as well as *resistance* to anything that threatens to allow the repressed to become conscious are already familiar indications of repressed impulses and perceptions.

A glance at everyday behavior shows it to be rife with contradiction. Especially striking are the *contradictions* between that which we consciously realize, and also desire, and our actual behavior. When understanding and aims, despite the best of intentions, do not correspond with actual behavior, this indicates that we are in the presence of an opposing unconscious desire. This desire, which remains unconscious to us, comes to dominate our behavior, making it inappropriate, irrational, and dysfunctional.

The most prominent examples are known from mental illness. Someone wants to write a term paper and has several good ideas but does not manage to bring pen to paper. If this difficulty cannot be resolved, we speak of a "writer's block," which, if we take the unconscious into account, is explained by a conflict between conscious desire and an opposing unconscious impulse, for example an unconscious performance anxiety. If it is possible to gain emotional access to the unconscious performance anxiety, the conflict abates and the person becomes able to put his thoughts on paper.

Something other than an unconscious performance anxiety standing in opposition to conscious desire can be present, perhaps an unconscious perfectionism in which no word brought to paper is good enough. Many conflicting unconscious impulses are imaginable that might explain such a psychological problem. A work disorder is only a small piece of a large spectrum of mental illnesses and states of suffering. The most well-known include depression, anxiety, obsessive compulsive disorders, and addiction, in which understanding and behavior diverge very dramatically, but also psychosomatic illness or problems of self-esteem. With all of these afflictions, it makes sense to assume that an unconscious opposing desire produces a conflict that forms the basis for the contradiction between understanding and behavior.

Most mental disorders are accompanied by the formation of symptoms and a level of distress that can be considered pathological. Precisely for that reason, those who are afflicted experience their behavior as disturbing and usually wish to be freed from their suffering. Yet, distress need not always be present when understanding and behavior contradict each other, and thereby point to the presence of an opposing unconscious desire.

To a large extent, our behavior is determined by our character formations, which we generally do not experience as disturbing (ego-syntonic). On the contrary, we tend to be at peace with how we are. Character formations determine our everyday conduct, distinguishing themselves by the uniform ways in which they shape the entire spectrum of our behavior. They often develop in the way that they do in order to keep an unconscious experience in check; this usually happens when a character trait or the entire orientation of the character strives for and demonstrates the exact opposite of the unconscious experience. Such character formations have a function similar to rationalizations. While rationalizations determine thought in such a way so that unconscious experience does not become conscious, character formations shape behavior so that neither the person concerned nor others can detect any conflicted behavior.

To illustrate with an example: a woman exhibits a pedantic character. Her thinking is doctrinaire, her work style, her interactions with others, her religiosity, her relationship with herself, her morality—in everything, she typically behaves pedantically, when it is neither necessary nor even appropriate. She herself is not bothered by this, she experiences herself as attentive, conscientious, and reliable. That's just the way she is—admittedly, to her partner's chagrin. What is unconscious for her in her pedantry, and what must remain unconscious—just to name *one* possibility—is a profound fear of loss which is so tied to her pedantry that she can no longer even sense it. She only knows that she would like to have everything under control and she believes that this is a good thing.

There are a number of very different indicators of the unconscious, some of which should at least be mentioned here: facial expressions, gestures, body posture, physical sensations, the way of walking, the gaze, blood flow in the skin, skin elasticity, muscle tension, tone of voice, the manner of speaking, the use of language, the formation of sounds, handwriting. All are a sort of seismograph for what is happening within us psychically and may point to unconscious states: conflicts, anxieties, shame, tension, pressure, anger, rage, interest, pleasure, infatuation, none of which may be conscious. The fact that these states are not conscious does not automatically mean that we cannot develop an awareness of them.

The same is true for the various psychic defense mechanisms that people employ in order to prevent certain inner perceptions from becoming conscious. They, too, are markers of the unconscious. Recognizing these mechanisms can help us become aware of repressed impulses and experiences in ourselves and others. Because of their particular importance as indicators of the unconscious, they are discussed in their own separate section.

Defensive strategies against becoming conscious of the unconscious

Defensive strategies are tasked with distorting certain repressed wishes, impulses, affects, and perceptions so that they can be satisfied or even expressed, while remaining unrecognized by the person employing those strategies (and sometimes even by those around him). We have already seen such a defensive function at work in rationalizations and character formations.

Certainly, the best known defensive strategy is *projection*. Projection can help us fend off our own impulses or perceptions from becoming conscious because we experience them as belonging to someone else. In this way, we remain in contact with what is repressed but we do not experience it as a part of ourselves. Such projections occur primarily with feelings and impulses experienced as negative or forbidden: I am not full of rage, rather the other is so destructive that I need to protect myself from him, or even drive out his destructiveness. Instead of experiencing my own hate, I feel myself hated by the other. Instead of experiencing my own guilt, I focus incessantly on the immense guilt of someone else, my spouse, the other driver, my parents who failed so miserably in my upbringing, etc.

Projection plays a central role in social and military conflicts. Without this demonization of an enemy, wars could not be waged or exploitative conditions upheld. We can most clearly recognize those repressed aspects of ourselves in projections by the way in which we feel ourselves completely free of the feelings and baseness that we so palpably sense in the other. Projection also plays a central role with those who always emphasize their own superiority and greatness, their flawlessness and perfection, and for that reason always need to devalue anything and everything that is not theirs or a reflection of themselves. Narcissistic self-idealization always correlates with a devaluation of the other as an inferior, primitive, asocial or incompetent being, whereby the devaluation indicates what is being projected: the narcissist's or narcissistic collective's feelings of inferiority, primitiveness, asocialness, and incompetence.

Projection differs from *displacement*. With displacement, what is repressed is still out in the open. Rage, hate, or even affection or tenderness are not kept out of conscious self-experience; only their trajectory shifts. Hostility, for example, is no longer directed toward the still-controlling father, but rather onto another father figure, a teacher or superior or a policeman as a representative of the "patriarchal" State. Tenderness cannot be expressed toward one's spouse, but is very easily lavished on the dog.

The *reversal into its opposite* is much harder to recognize, because the corresponding impulse or perception is more strongly distorted and the possibilities of becoming conscious better defended against. Here, usually destructive, avenging, enraged feelings are, so to speak, banished from the world in that they are reversed into their opposites. Instead of feeling murderous impulses, one can be exceedingly solicitous; instead of letting out all of one's frustration, one is overly friendly; instead of taking revenge for constant disparagements, one behaves always and at every moment appropriately and courteously. The behavior's excessive, exaggerated, demonstrative quality allows those around the person to recognize this reversal into its opposite more easily than the person can himself. From a psychoanalytic perspective, those who are never anything but sweet and understanding, who think and feel only positively, are not seen as saints but rather as people who no longer have access to their own self-assertive, aggressive feelings. They live in fear of being flooded and destroyed by them.

A defensive strategy related to displacement is *turning against oneself.* This is also usually deployed when aggressive feelings and impulses against other people are at play. If you depend on other people because you cannot live without them, or you have very ambivalent feelings toward them, you will not risk showing aggression toward them, since this would be sawing off the proverbial limb you are out on. What to do then with the reproaches, accusations, feelings of hate? You direct your aggression ultimately against yourself, in other words, you reproach and blame yourself, feel guilt, torment and restrain yourself in order to remain in good favor with those upon whom your (psychic) life appears to or actually does depend.

The above series of defensive strategies could be expanded to include many others. They should illustrate, however, how behavioral problems in the form of distorted and irrational actions point to the unconscious.

Understanding the unconscious

Unlike the above *indicators* of the unconscious that point us toward forces of which we are unaware, *roads* to the unconscious represent experiences and events through which we come into direct contact with the unconscious. The most notable of these phenomena include the dream, free association, parapraxis, transference, countertransference. (Other roads include symptoms and pathologies. Roads that did not carry much weight for Fromm, such as hypnotic trance states, drug-induced dissociative states, psychoses, or ecstatic states will not be discussed here.) In all of these phenomena, the unconscious makes itself known directly—it offers itself up. All that is required is to understand the unconscious's special language, logic, and modes of expression.

While our conscious perception and thought always rely on categories of space and time, permitting no logical contradictions, these categories play no role in the unconscious. Here, a paradoxical logic holds sway in which the most contradictory feelings, fantasies, impulses, and thoughts coexist. This singularity of unconscious perceptions ultimately led Fromm to understand the unconscious as the "whole" person, and not only in terms of the individual who embodies the entire spectrum of his possibilities: the unruly child, the infirm, the murderer, the saint, someone consumed by envy or someone consumed by love. The unconscious also represents the "universal" person, that is the human being who

> in any culture, *has all the potentialities*: he is the archaic man, the beast of prey, the cannibal, the idolater, and he is the being with the capacity for reason, for love, for justice. The content of the unconscious, then, is not just the good or the evil, the rational or the irrational; it is both; it is all that is human.
>
> *Humanism and Psychoanalysis,* 1963f

Inspired mainly by his engagement with Zen Buddhism, Fromm developed an understanding of unconscious perceptions during the course of his life in which the unconscious exceeds that which is repressed. Nevertheless, Fromm's roads to the unconscious are those that Freud already discovered.

> The great importance of the Freudian discovery of the possibility of being in touch with our unconscious is, precisely, that if we are in touch with it, then we (...) are in touch with the total man in us; and then, indeed, there is no more stranger. Further, there is no more judging of others in the sense that we consider ourselves superior to them. If we are in touch with our unconscious, then, indeed, we experience ourselves as we experience everybody else.
>
> *A New Humanism as a Condition for the One World,*
> 1992m [1962], p. 78

The dream as a road to the unconscious

The *dream* was for Freud—and remained also for Fromm—the "royal road" to understanding the unconscious. As we sleep, we largely withdraw our attention from the outside world and are not conscious of our existence. And yet, there is the inner activity of dreaming of which we become aware upon awakening. Freud had the idea that in dreams we are occupied with wishes, experiences, and ideas of which we cannot be conscious when we are awake, in other words, repressions. These repressions are articulated in fantastical dream stories, that is, in a language of images and symbols also found in poetry, myths, heroic epics, or in fairy tales.

With access to this symbolic language, we can decipher many dreams, and through the dream we gain access to an inner experience or state of which we are not conscious when we are awake. "It is the peculiarity of dreams that inner experiences are expressed as if they were sensory experiences, subjective states as if they were actions dealing with external reality. This interchange between the two modes of experience is the very essence of symbols, and particularly of the dream symbol" (*The Nature of Dreams*, 1949a, p. 45).

Dreams are something very intimate. Fromm shared numerous dreams in his writings but never one of his own. Most of the dreams on which Fromm published are from the patients of students whom he supervised (see especially the recollections of Fromm's students about his practice of psychoanalysis in Funk, 2009). The following illustrates how easily we can understand dreams if we open ourselves up to the language of images and symbols that they employ: "*I see a street of a big city; it is dawn; no one is on the street except an occasional drunk walking home; there is a drizzle of rain*" (*Is Man Lazy by Nature?*, 1991h [1974], p. 136). The primary point to realize is that every dream puts the internal state of the dreamer, above all the dreamer's feeling state, into images. "In the picture he has captured all elements in such a way that anyone listening to the dream can muster exactly the same feeling of loneliness, of separateness from all others, hopelessness, tiredness" (p. 136). Regardless of how the forty-year-old dreamer might describe his state when awake, the dream offers a precise and unvarnished description of his inner experience.

The close connection between dreaming and repressed perceptions that Freud saw was understood by Fromm and others to be only *one* possibility. With the recognition that the whole person is represented in the unconscious, Fromm followed a broadened understanding of the meaning of dreams (see also especially his book *The Forgotten Language. An Introduction to the Understanding of Dreams, Myths and Fairy Tales,* 1951a).

> There can be no doubt that many dreams express the fulfillment of irrational, asocial and immoral wishes which we repress successfully during the waking state. (...) But (...) we are often more intelligent, wiser and more moral in our sleep than in waking life. The reason for this is the ambiguous character of our social reality. (...) In sleep, no longer exposed to the "noise" of culture, we become awake to what we really feel and think. The genuine self can talk; it is often more intelligent and more decent than the pseudo self which seems to be "we" when we are awake.
>
> *The Nature of Dreams,* 1949a

Accordingly, Fromm believes that dreams often show our creative capacities more clearly than our waking state. "In dreams, the individual transcends the narrow boundaries of his society and becomes fully human" (*The Revolution of Hope,* 1968a, p. 71). For that reason alone, in the Frommian art of living understanding one's own dreams is a "must": "Our unconscious is the total man" (*A New Humanism as a Condition for the One World,* 1992m, p. 78). Fromm leaves no doubt about it: "'Dreams which are not understood are like letters which are not opened', says the Talmud, and this statement is undeniably true" (*The Nature of Dreams,* 1949a).

Free association as a road to the unconscious

When our unconscious perceptions stand in crass contradiction to our conscious experience, we readily try to distort and disguise the (latent) dream thought in the process of becoming aware of dreaming and the dream. Under certain circumstances, therefore, the manifest dream content accessible to us offers only laborious access to the unconscious. Freud attempted to address this difficulty by asking his patients to speak as freely and in as uncensored a manner as possible about what came to them in the present moment, regardless of whether or not these ideas made sense or fit the dream.

Freud called this road to the unconscious, which he developed following his experiments with hypnosis, *free association*. Sensitivity to that which occurs to one in the moment is, in addition to dreams, a separate and often very successful pathway to the unconscious. With free association, it is important to ignore the customary rules of respectability, disregarding if one's thoughts seem intelligent or even worth mention, or if they even have anything to do with the topic at hand. The point is for someone to

> leave the realm of conventional, rational thought, and permit himself to voice ideas which are not determined by the rules of normal, conventional thinking. If he does this, ideas emerge (...) which are not part of his official personality, but which are the language of this dissociated, hidden personality.
>
> *Remarks on the Problem of Free Association,* 1955d, p. 33

Fromm illustrates free association with the following example from his therapeutic practice:

> A thought (a) deals with a friend toward whom the patient feels consciously very friendly, although in fact he felt jealous on hearing the night before of his friend's promotion; association (b), apparently without connection, deals with an incident the patient read about in the morning's paper: a man was killed by a rival; association (c) recalls the patient's life in school, when he felt very unhappy at having been demoted from first to second place.
>
> *Psychoanalysis,* 1955e, p. 368

If we try to understand all three associations, it is easy to see that they share a common, recurring theme and feeling. All three show an envious, rivalrous animosity between two men, which obviously also determines the consciously amicable relationship with the friend. Here, it is also crucial to confront the possibility that this patient, despite all protests to the contrary, struggles with an unconscious destructiveness.

If this were spoken to directly, the patient would presumably put up resistance: "the patient may begin to talk about trivial things, feel sleepy, get discouraged, angry or what not" (p. 369).

In therapy, the request at the beginning of a session to say simply what comes to mind is often understood by patients as an invitation to chatter or complain incessantly about their unresponsive mother or their violent father. In so doing, they are often only living out their resistance to becoming conscious of what they have repressed. For that reason, Fromm defined free association more precisely as "spontaneous" association (which is how it was originally meant) and combined this with concentration exercises. (See *Remarks on the Problem of Free Association*, 1955d, p. 32.) Since this pathway to the unconscious also has meaning in non-therapeutic contexts, it should be clarified further.

When working with *spontaneous* association, it is important to use the immediacy of the moment, which allows no room for reflection. We see this first of all in the direct request: "Tell me what is in your mind *right now*" (p. 34). It can be even more effective to combine spontaneous association with a request for concentration: "Now, concentrate on the picture of your father, and tell me what is the first thing that comes to your mind" (p. 34). Fromm also combined spontaneous association with concentration exercises in which he asked his counterpart to close his eyes and think about nothing until after a few minutes when he would say "Now!" With eyes still closed, his counterpart would then say what was going through his mind at that exact moment. "The advantage of this technique is that by this short period of concentration the patient's conventional thought process is by-passed, as it were, and usually the associations come from a deeper level of the unconscious" (p.33).

With this method, the patient saw himself first as a prisoner of war crying for help, completely alone and abandoned by others. In a second image, the man then saw himself astride a white warhorse, leading a regiment into battle.

> Actually, this was a patient whose whole personality was split between a person who, in his social relations or in his love relations, was a helpless person feeling lonely and powerless; in his professional

relations as a surgeon, he was sure of his authority, fearless and competent with an element of grandiosity.

p. 35

The technique of "spontaneous" association practiced by Fromm differs not only from the usual therapeutic practice of "free" association, but also from work with daydreams and fantasies, which reveal much more about those wishes closer to consciousness that are not so easily admitted than about unconscious perceptions and states.

Parapraxis as a road to the unconscious

By way of introduction, here is an example that Fromm liked to tell:

> Not long ago I received a visit from a colleague who I know does not particularly like me. Indeed, I was rather amazed that he wanted to come see me at all. He rang the doorbell; I opened the door; he held out his hand and said cheerfully: "Goodbye." Translation: His unconscious mind was already wishing he could be gone. He had not been looking forward to this visit, and he revealed that by saying "goodbye" instead of "hello."
>
> *Psychology for Nonpsychologists*, 1974a, p. 74

Because of convention, he could not give in to his unconscious feeling, and yet his aversion to the visit asserted itself behind his back, as it were. Parapraxes are especially impressive in showing how unconscious desire and conscious intention can be in conflict, while the unconscious blazes its own "unintended" trail. For exactly this reason, parapraxes offer good access to the unconscious. "The excuse 'I didn't mean it' is the traditional excuse for something which shows that one didn't have the intention" (*Therapeutic Aspects of Psychoanalysis*, 1991d [1974], p. 74). Ever since Freud described parapraxes at length in his book *The Psychopathology of Everyday Life* (Freud, 1901), this excuse no longer holds. Unconsciously, this was precisely what one intended.

The most common parapraxes are slips of the tongue. But the spectrum of possible kinds of parapraxes is enormously broad. It extends from slips of the tongue to slips of the pen, from forgetting things to losing things, from misreading, mishearing, and misplacing to mixing up, messing up, and ultimately, mishaps. Of course, there is not always an unconscious intention behind every parapraxis. There are linguistic characteristics (anticipated and lingering sounds), states of excitement, fatigue, or a lack of concentration, which may cause a parapraxis or foster one.

One can best recognize a "Freudian slip" by the (resistant) reaction of the one who "makes" the mistake. The person wants to correct and undo it immediately, he swears that he meant the exact opposite of what he just said or did, and launches into long explanations (rationalizations) about why he is completely sure that he did not mean what just "slipped out."

Some parapraxes occur repeatedly, for example losing one's keys or wallet (with bank cards and ID) or getting into accidents. They become a symptom, and, for example, point to an unconscious loss of identity or a harmful or self-harming (masochistic) aggression that can only be expressed through parapraxes.

Parapraxes can be completely hidden and yet offer much insight into a person's unconscious. They can also be seen in trivial and "meaningless" actions. Often, they consist solely of an "also" that one inserts by mistake into a description of somebody else and thereby inadvertently communicates that the speaker, too, is implicated. Parapraxes can have dire consequences, for example a driver overlooks a pedestrian and runs him over, or someone stumbles and is badly injured.

Often, parapraxes reveal themselves in expressions to the contrary: when someone gushes about a good relationship and remarks that the future of the relationship is "hopeless, um—hopeful," he first speaks a truth of which he is not conscious, only to correct himself immediately. It is important with such parapraxes not to talk them away or be swallowed up with shame, and avoid any future contact with the concerned parties. Instead, parapraxis can be understood as a means for self-understanding and as a chance for more honest relations between people. This naturally presumes a sort of interpersonal contact that does not deploy parapraxis as a "weapon" against the other or as "proof" of his or her evil intentions or poor character, but rather as an offer by the unconscious for a direct encounter.

Transference as a road to the unconscious

For therapeutic work, the most important road to the unconscious is transference. As Fromm noted, Freud already observed "that his patients often developed ideas about him and reactions to him which were not founded at all on reality. One patient might see him as an all-powerful or all-wise man; another as a weak and timid man; a third as a sinister ogre" (*Psychoanalysis*, 1955e, p. 369).

Freud also observed that the patients in question had had similar experiences with people who were important for them in their childhood. At the same time, patients would repeat these experiences with their husband, father-in-law, or wife or mother-in-law, in large part regardless of these family members' actual personalities. Childhood experiences are unconsciously transferred onto those people with whom the patient has relationships today. The more intensively the therapeutic relationship develops, the more directly one can come into contact with the patient's childhood experiences (wishes, fears, conflicts, frustrations, etc.).

Fromm took on the phenomenon of transference in order to give it a much more comprehensive meaning as a pathway to a person's unconscious. Transferences for Fromm play a major role in the life of every human being. The more dependent and helpless man is, or experiences himself to be, the more frequently transferences occur. This, of course, applies first and foremost to the small child who could not survive without a supportive, protective environment and close-knit, empathic caregivers. The more people become capable of protecting, supporting, and understanding themselves, the more their need decreases for other people to provide such existentially reinforcing and buttressing experiences.

In several respects, even an adult human being is and remains dependent and in need, and therefore also has a tendency to overcome his own helplessness with external means, through those people and institutions superior in power and strength. This existential situation is, of course, exploited by economic and social forces. These forces keep people dependent and helpless by making them believe that they can better overcome their powerlessness and helplessness by expecting their problems to be solved by powerful and potent leaders, idols, and institutions, opportunities for consumption or entertainment, media, or search engines. In other words, they transfer their own strengths on to them.

For Fromm,

> transference is a result of the failure in one's own freedom and thereby is the result of the need to find an idol to worship, to believe in in order to overcome one's fear and uncertainty about the world. The adult human being is in a way not less helpless than the child. He *could* be less helpless if he or she grows up to be a fully independent, developed human being, but if he or she doesn't then indeed he or she is just as helpless as a child, because he or she sees himself or herself surrounded by a world over which he or she has no influence, which he doesn't understand, which leaves him in uncertainty and fear and therefore while a child seeks an adult—the father or mother—for, let us say, biological reasons, the grown-up person seeks the same for social and historical reasons.
>
> *Therapeutic Aspects of Psychoanalysis*, 1991d [1974], p. 119

The phenomenon of transference and the production of a "transference neurosis" within the therapeutic setting can certainly be helpful in establishing emotional access to earlier experiences of relationships that have not yet been worked through and are for that reason repressed. In this case, the goal is to remove the actual transferences from their breeding ground. For Fromm, however, the Freudian discovery of transference first takes on its true meaning only when it is seen as an everyday phenomenon in which the perception of relatedness to others and oneself is not based in reality and therefore irrational. Fundamentally, "what we are dealing with is the need of a person to have another person to fulfill this need. For instance, if I feel weak, uncertain, afraid of risks, afraid of decisions—I may want to find a person who is certain, who is prompt, who is powerful, in whom I can take refuge" (p. 120).

In the Frommian understanding of transference, the emphasis is on the satisfaction of one's *own* needs, which one expects from others. In the process, our own world of wishes, needs, and fears distorts our perception of the other person.

For Fromm, therefore, transference is

> one of the most common reasons for human *error and conflict* in sizing up reality. It makes us see the world through the glasses of our own wishes and fears and consequently makes us confuse illusion with reality. We do not see other people as they really are but the way we want them to be or fear that they are. Those illusions about other people take the place of reality. We do not perceive others as they are but as they appear to us to be, and when we react to them, we are reacting not to real human beings in their own right but to products of our imagination.
>
> *Psychology for Nonpsychologists*, 1974a, pp. 78–79

It is not enough to see transference solely as a repetition of childhood experiences; rather, it should be generally understood as "the mobilization of the ubiquitous desire for an idol" (*The Dialectic Revision of Psychoanalysis*, 1990f [1969], p. 48).

If one understands the phenomenon of transference as Fromm did, then it makes far more sense to focus our entire attention on which wishes and anxieties people transfer to those things that they sought, longed for, or feared: spouses, (magic) helpers, political, religious, and social institutions, leaders, therapists, idols, opportunities for consumption and entertainment. The simple fact and strength of transference allow us to recognize a usually unconscious powerlessness in people who are incapable of living on their own and relying on their own strength. Beyond that, uncovering what is transferred illuminates actual, but usually unconscious, states of need, helplessness, disappointment, and powerlessness.

Without doubt, the phenomenon of transference, and the distorted perception of self and others that accompanies it, hinder any direct encounter. On the other hand, an awareness of transference makes direct access to the unconscious possible—to one's own unconscious as well as to the unconscious of others.

The above chapter illustrates how for Fromm the inclusion of the unconscious is indispensable for any art of living. There are two reasons for this: the unconscious can be repressed. But that which is repressed hinders any direct encounter with the self and the other because it is always accompanied by a loss of energy and a limited, because distorted, perception. The unconscious can also liberate energies because the unconscious represents the whole person, including those aspects and energies at particular social and historical moments that are not allowed to become conscious and develop. Every person is born with thousands of possibilities and talents capable of development. Which of these actually come into play depends, according to Fromm, far more on social than on personal circumstances—that is, on which feelings, impulses, and energies an economy and society can and cannot use for its own functioning.

The following chapter is dedicated to a second fundamental insight that is just as indispensable for any art of living as access to the unconscious: the insight that the individual exists as nothing other than a *social* being and that this is represented within one's own structure of psychic formation. How did Fromm arrive at this view? Here, too, the biographical context in which Fromm developed this core idea of his art of living should prove of interest.

Figure 3 Fromm at Davos, 1932. © Lit Fromm Estate.

2

The Individual as a Social Being

Erich Fromm—an only child becomes a psychoanalyst of society

Growing up an only child certainly shapes one differently than growing up with brothers and sisters, where one might be the oldest or youngest or somewhere in between an array of siblings. Fromm grew up as an only child in Frankfurt's Westend neighborhood. He was in especially close contact with his father's side of the family in which there were very few children. Here, again, Erich usually found himself alone as a child facing a generally older world of adults, as Fromm's father was the second youngest of a total of ten siblings, almost all of whom remained childless. Only with Charlotte from Berlin, a maternal cousin three years his senior, did Erich enjoy a warm, sibling-like connection, when she was allowed to spend her vacation in Frankfurt with her Aunt Rosa, Erich's mother, and her cousin, Erich. The twelve- and thirteen-year-old Erich could also debate for hours on end with a young Galician named Oskar Süßmann, whom his father had hired to work in his berry wine shop on Liebigstraße.

In addition, Fromm's father was at anxious and jealous pains to see that his boy Erich—except for his attendance at the Wöhler Gymnasium—was exposed to as few contacts outside the family as possible. His father, so said the 79-year-old Fromm in an interview, "had no fears about himself but had a neurotic anxiety about me and as an only child it was a very bad situation (...) He liked me as a little baby but he was jealous of all the friends I had" (*Interview*, 2000f [1979]).

Fromm's general sense as a child and adolescent that he often confronted a world not his own was compounded by the fact that he grew up in a Jewish family. When Fromm was born, it had barely been forty years since the Jews of Frankfurt were allowed to live outside of the Jewish ghetto and enter into certain professions that had thus far been prohibited for Jews. Yet the previously enforced social orientation toward one's own religious community continued to determine the social behavior of most Jewish families. Being Jewish still meant confronting a social majority who considered them to be foreign (see Funk, 1983, pp. 7–13).

What's more: his father's side followed a long tradition of distancing themselves from those Jewish groups who aspired to assimilate into the liberal, Christian middle class. The adolescent Erich Fromm was especially proud of his family's strict adherence to Orthodox Jewish religious practice. But this practice also made Fromm feel alien:

> [I lived] really half in this world of the authentic tradition of ancient Judaism and half in the modern world: I went to school in Frankfurt and had the same influences as every other young German at the time. But I remained very much alone with this: not only because as a Jew in Germany one always occupies a sort of special position, if by no means an unpleasant one. But, I also remained alone because I never felt entirely at home in the world in which I lived, but also not in the old world of traditions, as this, too, was also not my daily experience.
>
> *Interview,* 1977i

The above quotation is taken from a television interview conducted by Jürgen Lodemann and Micaela Lämmle in 1976. It contains the young Fromm's basic question in a pointed formulation: he not only understands that he, as an individual, confronts a world that is not his own; he also recognizes that he must find a way in which he can *live between these two worlds.* Next to the psychological question—"how is it possible that people think, feel, and act so irrationally?"—this became the second overarching question of his entire life's work.

Because of his own existential situation, on the one hand Fromm burned with interest to find out how to be alone and an individual, without remaining alone; on the other hand, he needed to answer the question of how one can adapt to society and be with the other, without losing one's individuality and uniqueness. Man can only bridge the entirely personal and individual world on one side, and the public and social world on the other, if he can preserve his own individuality and uniqueness *as well as* do justice to society's demands and possibilities. Fromm's second fundamental question had to do with the relationship between the individual and society.

Biographically speaking, Fromm attempted to answer the second question first. The focus of his sociological studies with Alfred Weber in Heidelberg (1919–1924) was his dissertation on the sociology of the Diaspora Jews entitled *The Jewish Law*. In this study, he wanted to know the meaning that the lived Torah had for Jews living together in the Diaspora and whose cohesion as a social group was not provided for by state or other public institutions (see 1989b [1922], GA XI, pp. 19–126). As a sociologist, Fromm was not primarily interested in the function that institutions had for social cohesion. Rather, he pursued the question of what allowed people to think, feel, and act similarly when they had no such exterior institutional structure. In so doing, he came to the realization that the lived form of ethics or the ethos, internalized through religious practice, provides the sense of social cohesion. We could also say that Fromm was already using a sociopsychological approach in his dissertation without possessing his own psychological theory. Only after his dissertation in 1922 did he become familiar with and develop these ideas through his relationship with Frieda Reichmann.

Presumably what contributed more than Fromm's studies and dissertation to his ideas about the relationship between the individual and society was his private instruction from 1920 to 1925 with the teacher Shlomo Baruch Rabinkow at 14 Rahmengasse in Heidelberg. This Talmudic scholar of the Chabad Hasidic tradition had written only one single extensive piece, albeit it with the telling title "Individual and Community in Judaism" (Rabinkow, 1929). About Rabinkow, Fromm wrote:

> I was his student for about five or six years, and if I remember correctly I visited him at that time almost daily. The bulk of the time was occupied with studying Talmud, the rest with studying certain

philosophical writings of Maimonides, the Rav's *Tanya*, Weiss's Jewish history, and a discussion of sociological problems. He took great interest and was very helpful in my doctoral dissertation, which was a sociopsychological analysis of the Karaites, the Hasidic movement, and the Jewish Reform movement. (...) Rabinkow influenced my life more than any other man, perhaps, and although in different forms and concepts, his ideas have remained alive in me. (...) He was a man with whom one could never, even at the first meeting, feel oneself a stranger. It was as if one were continuing a conversation or relationship which had always existed. And that was necessarily so, because of his attitude. There was no polite small talk, no careful probing, no questioning appraisal of his visitor, but an immediate openness, concern, participation. (...) I was never shy in front of Rabinkow. I do not remember a single instance in which I felt afraid of his judgment, of what he might say about this or of that, that he might "judge" me; nor did he try to influence me, to tell me what to do, to admonish me. All his influence was his being, his example, although he was the last man to want to present an example. He was just himself.

Reminiscences of Shlomo Barukh Rabinkow, 1987a, p. 101

I deliberately quote Fromm's memories of Rabinkow in such great detail here because they show that Fromm experienced Rabinkow in much the same way that I experienced Fromm fifty years later: as a person who is capable of a direct encounter (see Funk, 1992). Fromm and other students of Rabinkow were fascinated that he practiced a strict religious life and was at the same time completely free and independent. In his teachings, Rabinkow advocated a radically humanistic stance while seeing "Judaism as a system with emphasis on equality, justice, and the dignity of the individual" (p. 103). Individual self-determination—the freedom to be who *he* wanted to be—was more important than any expectations set by social or religious communities.

The psychiatrist Nahum Goldman, who was also one of Rabinkow's students, illuminated with the following incident how the relationship between the individual and society in favor of individual freedom was resolved. When Rabinkow was once asked by a Neo-Orthodox Jew, who felt that all male Jews must have beards, why he was clean-shaven, he countered, not without humor:

> Suppose I live out my life without a beard. When I die and come before God's throne in the next and better world, the worst that can happen is that He will say to me, "Jew Rabinkov, where is your beard?" To which I will have to reply, "Lord, here is a Jew without a beard." But when you appear before God, He'll ask, "Beard, where is your Jew?"
>
> Goldman, 1969, p. 106

Rabinkow's exemplary freedom fundamentally put into question Fromm's previous practice of defining his individual interests by the expectations of his forefathers' religion. Without Rabinkow's humanistic practice, Fromm could hardly have implemented a break with the orthodox religion of his forbears on that Passover in 1926. Thus, it was not only contact with Freud's teachings about the unconscious that led Fromm to this liberating act and to a new personal definition of the relationship between the individual and society.

In the following years, Fromm's personal liberation also led to a new and very fruitful scholarly orientation, especially with regard to the question of the relationship between the individual and society. Until then, he believed that one could find what was individual and unique about oneself by practicing Orthodox Judaism, and he had seen himself in conflict with bourgeois, non-Jewish society. Now he could see how much he had allowed society, in the form of a religious Jewish practice, to take precedence over his individual needs and interests.

Without doubt, Fromm's psychoanalytic experiences in the mid-1920s contributed considerably to this shift. Psychoanalysis is concerned with the liberation of the individual from the internalized demands of society that run counter to his needs and interests. These individual desires stem from instinctual demands, according to Freud. For that reason, the individual was understood as a creature of drives whose foremost goal was their satisfaction, while society primarily tried to restrain and limit these desires.

In principle, Freudian psychoanalysis with its drive theory fit into the "modern" paradigm of contemporary thinking at the time, according to which the interests of society stand in opposition to the interests of the individual. This modern opposition between the individual and society was of essential significance. It made it possible to overcome the "premodern" paradigm in which the individual experiences himself primarily as part of a collective. This strong bond with the community had been necessary for survival.

The modern position of the individual who stands in opposition to society was the precondition for standing up to social forces in the name of individual liberties and basic rights. Psychoanalysis finds its rightful place in this history of liberation, as Freudian drive theory led to ambivalent assessments of the relationship between the individual and society. For the purposes of a peaceful and social coexistence, it is completely justified and necessary for society to push the individual to renounce those desires that run counter to the interests of society. Thus, aggressive and egoistic instinctual demands should indeed be suppressed, repressed, or sublimated. On the other hand, instinctual sexual demands should be respected in the face of society's claims of authority. Psychoanalysis understood itself in its first decades as a liberation movement, freeing people from the sexual paternalism of Victorian moral sensibilities. Freudian psychoanalysis contributed fundamentally to our modern understanding of the conflict between the individual and society.

On a scholarly level, the history of the demarcation of the individual from society led to the development and separation of entirely new branches of research. The social sciences and psychology were born. The former chose society, the latter the individual as its preferred object of study. With these divisions, however, the wish arose for an interdisciplinary academic concept. One emerged in the 1920s at the "Institute for Social Research" in Frankfurt, which since 1929 was headed by Max Horkheimer. It was at this Institute—later known as the "Frankfurt School"—to which Fromm belonged from 1930 to 1939, that the specifically Frommian interest in a new definition of the relation between the individual and society found ample stimulation. The Institute members, not only Max Horkheimer but also especially

Herbert Marcuse, Leo Löwenthal, and Friedrich Pollock, were inspired by Marxist social theory. Marx's theories described the alienating effects of economic and social conditions on people and the possibilities for overcoming them. Fromm's assignment at the Institute was to integrate insights from Freudian psychoanalysis into interdisciplinary research and to develop theories and methods that could link sociological and psychological ideas in a unique *sociopsychological* approach. As early as 1929 in the short contribution *Psychoanalysis and Sociology*, he had already sketched out such an approach: "Psychoanalysis interprets the development of individuals precisely in terms of their relationship to their closest and most intimate surroundings; it considers the psychological apparatus as formed most decisively by these relationships" (1929a).

Fromm's idea was to reconnect the individual and society by ascribing a central role to society in the shaping of instinctual impulses ("formed most decisively"). He still thought entirely in the categories of Freudian drive theory and described, in what is probably one of his most important early writings with the prophetic title *The Method and Function of an Analytic Social Psychology* (1932a), how a society has a "libidinal structure" in addition to an economic, social, political and cultural structure. "The libidinal structure of a society is the medium through which the economy exerts its influence on man's intellectual and mental manifestations" (1932a, p. 132). This "libidinal structure" can be recognized in every individual who is socialized in this manner.

Fromm provided empirical evidence for this sociopsychological approach with field research, which he had already initiated by 1929, but which was first published in 1980 under the title *The Working Class in Weimar Germany. A Psychological and Sociological Study* (1980a). Fromm wanted to show that people's political thought can also be a rationalization, using as an example those in the working class who expressly identified themselves as politically on the Left. On the basis of freely formulated answers to an open questionnaire, he could show that in the majority of cases revolutionary declarations did not correspond with revolutionary instinctual impulses. Instead, despite the leftist thinking, actions and real behavior were based on more or less unconscious and reactionary instinctual impulses. The evaluation indicated that only 15 percent of over 600 people interviewed thought in revolutionary ways that actually corresponded to their libidinal structure. In retrospect, Fromm also realized with his study why resistance to Hitler's seizure of power could not be expected on the part of the leftist working class, and why a majority of them sympathized with National Socialism, even becoming members of the Nazi party. (See *Social Character in a Mexican Village*, 1970b, pp. 24–29.)

The fruitfulness of Fromm's sociopsychological approach is most obvious, however, in his studies of the authoritarian character. The question of authority was the most important topic at the Institute for Social Research between 1930 and 1936. Fromm shows in his "Social-Psychological Part" (*Sozialpsychologischer Teil*, 1936a, GA I, S. 139–187) of *Studies on Authority and Family* (edited by Horkheimer) how sadomasochistic impulses are very much the result of an authoritarian, capitalist economy's influence on libidinal structure. Many people's behavior is determined by their authoritarian character, which tends to kowtow to those above and browbeat those below.

With his sociopsychological approach, Fromm had found a way to redefine the relationship between the individual and society. He understood the individual to be a socialized human being, in so far as we can discern in many people, along with their particular uniqueness, the unifying libidinal structure of society. (Because of this, instead of the libidinal structure of society, Fromm would later speak of the "social character" in contrast to "individual character.") From a psychological perspective, society as such does not exist for Fromm; there are only individuals with the same or similar impulses, values, and behavioral characteristics, who, on the basis of these commonalities, can be understood as a society or a social class, group, stratum, or milieu. "Society and the individual are not 'opposite' to each other. *Society is nothing but living, concrete individuals, and the individual can live only as a social human being*" (*Man's impulse structure and its relation to culture*, 1992e [1937]; see Funk, 2000a). This may also explain why Fromm, with his doctorate in sociology and his sociopsychological approach to understanding society, made few friends among the sociologists.

Although by 1932 Fromm was already very convinced by his new understanding of the relationship between the individual and society, he simultaneously became very doubtful about Freudian drive theory as a metatheory that could explain this relationship. Did all conscious and unconscious emotional forces experienced as instinctual really stem from a human nature based on instinct? In 1936, Fromm at last took some time to write an essay in which he spelled out his divergences from Freud. On December 18, 1936, he wrote about this to his Institute colleague, Karl August Wittfogel, who was living in China at the time:

> I worked over my fundamental reexamination of Freud. The core of the argument is when I try to demonstrate that those urges which motivate social activities are not, as Freud supposes, sublimations of sexual instincts, but rather products of social processes or, to be more precise, reactions to certain circumstances in which human beings need to satisfy their instincts. These urges (. . .) differ in principle from the natural factors, namely the drives to satisfy hunger, thirst, and sexual desire. While all human beings and animals have these in common, the others are specifically human productions, and not to be understood biologically, but rather as in the context of the social practice of living.
>
> Erich Fromm Archive, Tübingen

In this essay, Fromm illustrates why impulses such as frugality, hate, or sadism do not stem from a pregenital sexual drive, but rather have their basis in economic and social demands and constellations, and thereby originate in the social relatedness of human beings. Fromm's actual critique lies in his understanding of man not as a being who must satisfy libidinal derivatives of an innate drive, but rather as a being who, because of his particular biological situation, had to develop his own forms of relatedness to reality, to other people, and to himself. Not the satisfaction of drives, but rather the existential need to relate, leads to a broad spectrum of psychic urges and impulses that are typical of human beings.

Fromm's different approach of sociopsychology met with unanimous rejection at the Institute for Social Research. One of his publications was categorically turned down. Only in 1990, in the New York Public Library, did I come across this essay and publish it (see *Man's impulse structure and its relation to culture*, 1992e [1937]). Fromm remained alone with his psychoanalytic approach to society. In 1939, the Institute finally terminated his position.

The following sections show the possibilities inherent in Fromm's new definition of the relationship between the individual and society, namely when an explanatory framework of drive theory is replaced by a theory of relatedness.

What makes a father beat his children?

In the previous chapter, to illustrate the repression of a sadistic impulse we used Fromm's example of a sadistic father who, without feeling sadistic, beats and abuses his children. Instead, he only senses that he does his duty, while preventing his children from doing anything bad. The feeling that he does something good by beating his children serves as a rationalization for the father, which helps him to repress his sadistic wish—this is why he doesn't sense anything sadistic in the beating.

On the basis of this example, we now want to ask about the origins of such sadism on the father's part. And, we will also want to ask how it is possible that the father does not sense this sadism, but rather only has the feeling that he is doing something good for his children when he beats them.

A preliminary psychological answer is certainly that the (not conscious but enacted) impulse to do violence to his children is rooted in his own childhood experiences. His father had also beaten him and, like thousands of others, was convinced that beating was a tried and true parenting method. He never learned or saw anything different.

A psychoanalytic answer would add that, as a child who experienced an unbearable feeling of powerlessness in the face of his own violent father, the father could only cope with being defenseless by identifying with the aggressor. And thus, he developed a sadistic tendency and became abusive. A psychoanalytic explanation is certainly helpful if one wants to interrupt this sort of "inheritance." It makes clear that the sadistic wish to beat can develop when someone is made to feel deeply powerless and defenseless.

Freud originally saw in sadism a partial component of the libido, and later a mixture of Eros and the death drive. In both theories, Freud understands sadism as the result of *instinctual drives* that originate within human beings. Social influences also play an important role in Freud's theories. They can lead to the suppression, repression, or satisfaction of a drive, even possibly contributing to its sublimation. In other words, social influences can be directed toward goals that are helpful and beneficial. For example, Freud believed that a good surgeon has sublimated parts of his sadistic instincts. Fundamentally, however, Freud saw sadism as an expression of our instinctual nature, the manifestations of which may be managed but never truly dispelled.

With his essay of 1937, Fromm attempted to offer a fundamentally different answer as to the origins of the abusive father's sadistic impulse. For Fromm, man's basic problem is not his instinctual nature and the question of drive satisfaction, but rather his relationship to reality, which forces him to adopt socially acceptable patterns of relatedness in order not to remain isolated. What society needs for its own functioning—its economic, social, and cultural requirements as well as its values—is what the individual must make his own and must himself want, if he wants to experience himself as belonging to a particular society. Society thus finds its way into each individual, who now does what a society needs for its own success with pleasure and with passion. At the same time, the impacts of this process of assimilation and socialization within the individual enable a psychological exploration of society.

The question still remains as to where the father's sadism originates according to Fromm, and how it is possible that the father still feels good about it. The sadistic father beats, Fromm might answer, because during his socialization a socially demanded and desired impulse was formed within him. For Fromm, beating is a typical relic of an authoritarian society in which the exercise of authority is carried out by violence and punishment, and in which *common sense* dictates that beatings have never hurt anyone and punishment is necessary for raising honorable and obedient citizens. What rationalizations enable on the personal level, ideology enables on the social level in the form of *common sense*, as well as stereotypes and systems: it ensures that beating and punishment are viewed as something normal, good, and even necessary.

If we cannot attribute the emergence of the sadistic impulse to drives that originate within human beings, but rather find it to be shaped by society, then we must ask: how does the impulse develop within the individual? A naive formulation might be: How does society enter into the individual and where is it located within him? We now know much more about the significance that the first years of life have for mental development and how dependent these interactions are on those caregivers who occupy the roles of mother and father.

The individual as socialized being

For Fromm, every human being is always already related to reality and to others. Insights from psychiatry—and here, above all, from psychiatrist Harry Stack Sullivan—support Fromm's approach. The most severe psychological states of suffering—such as schizophrenia—arise when people can no longer relate to their given and expected reality and therefore develop a "mad" method of relating. They do this because no one can exist without relationships. The question is not therefore *whether* we are related, but rather the *manner* in which we are. Every person always lives with only a limited choice of patterns of relatedness that develop and shift according to age, family, intellectual, psychological, and physical development, professional and social status, etc.

Like Freud, Fromm is convinced that the basic forms of relatedness—today we speak of "patterns of attachment"—develop in childhood, namely through the experiences of relationship that the infant, the toddler, and the child have with their close "relations." These close relations, in the form of mother, father, grandparents, and siblings, among others, shape the child through their individual personality in very different ways, and yet simultaneously they, too, are beings shaped by society, passing on their own social imprint through their very similar patterns of attachment, values, educational ideas, and styles. The caregivers—in the past, one simply spoke of the "family"—are therefore always at the same time also agents of those socially demanded and desired patterns of attachment that make the child into a socialized being.

The family is "itself the product of a particular social system" (*Psychoanalysis and Sociology*, 1929a, p. 38) and thus "the medium through which the society or the social class stamps its specific structure on the child, and hence on the adult. *The family is the psychological agency of society*" (*The Method and Function of an Analytic Social Psychology*, 1932a, p. 117). For Fromm, following this other definition of the relation between the individual and society, the family is not a place that protects one from social influences. Instead, it is the primary space in which society, through socialized parents, exerts its influence. Of course, today this medium can no longer be characterized simply as "family," given the way electronic media have conquered the nursery over the last several decades with their emphasis on the visual and their fantastic possibilities of connectivity. Yet even media, with their enacted and virtual worlds, convey symbolizations of those values and relationship patterns that a society requires for its own functioning.

Through the help of caregivers and electronic media, society already exerts its formative influence in early childhood. Long before the child has any social consciousness and long before the child is able to distinguish between social demands and his own, he exhibits behavior that originates in socially molded patterns of relatedness.

No one is ever exclusively a "child" of his society. The emphasis on social influence does not mean that very singular circumstances and experiences cannot play a decisive role in the life of each individual. For example—when a child is four, her parents' marriage finally collapses after long, quarrelsome discussions; a two-year-old's unfortunate fall requires a hospital stay; during the first five years of life Grandma was always there, she could always tell the most wonderful stories and she always had something good to eat; there was a dog who had an especially soft coat; and one's sister was a friend in whom one could confide everything—all of these individual experiences of self and relationship shape a person as well.

Even if, according to Fromm, the individual is always already a socialized being, he is never simply a reflection of the demands of the social community. As a consequence, we need to distinguish between the individual and social aspects of his formation.

Until now, we have pursued with Fromm the question as to how society "enters into" the individual. But we have not yet elaborated on *where* it is located within the individual. Rather, we have spoken relatively vaguely of "patterns of relatedness" and socially molded "emotional forces" and "passions." Fromm developed a clear conception of the psychic structural formation through which society exerts its influence on the individual. In so doing, he made use of Freud's expanded idea of "character," speaking of social character to describe the psychic structure that allows us to think, feel, and act with pleasure and passion, and through which the behavior of the individual contributes to the stability and success of society.

The meaning of character formations

The Frommian idea of social character is linked with the already familiar psychoanalytic or dynamic concept of character. According to this concept, character represents a structure formed by emotional forces or impulses (character traits) within the psyche of one or many people. Endowed with psychic energy, this structure imparts a specific trajectory and focus (orientation) to concrete behavior. Unlike most theories of personality, a dynamic theory of character presumes that behavior is driven by interest; in other words, behavior exhibits a conscious or unconscious aim and therefore possesses an emotional-affective dimension.

A psychoanalytic explanatory framework positing a psychodynamic understanding of character, in which a psychic structural formation imparts an emotional-affective orientation to behavior, arrives at conclusions very similar to those of neurobiological behavioral theories. These theories speak of the necessary development of stable synapses and highly differentiated neural networks connected to emotional centers, or of psychologically empirical theories of behavior and learning that explain conscious and unconscious behavioral systems with different memory formations.

In psychodynamic terms, we always speak of character-oriented behavior when we see that someone strives for something with his behavior, which means his behavior cannot be understood only as a reflex or a reaction to a particular stimulus. Moreover, we recognize behavior conditioned by character because it appears "typical" or "characteristic." The conscious and unconscious impulse or energies that determine behavior make it *uniform* (one thinks, feels, and acts the same way in different situations), *consistent* (coherent and "in tune," predictable and reliable), and *inflexible*. The impulse attempts to assert itself through this behavior, even when a situation would call for a completely different sort of behavior, for example, when certain actions are so unexpected that the behavior is inappropriate, dysfunctional, or plainly counterproductive.

All of this suggests that our thoughts, feelings, and actions are in large part determined by inner impulses and passionate strivings that we call "character traits." If someone is frugal, this can be an appropriate reaction to a real situation. If someone has no money, he is wise to spend sparingly. However, when someone has ample resources and still cannot indulge himself or share with others, then his frugal behavior is driven by a particular character trait. The person in question sees this as a positive character trait, that is, he is simply a frugal person who doesn't spend his money frivolously; others, however, correctly identify him as having a "miserly character trait." The fact that the person declares his miserly behavior to be a positive thriftiness only shows that he is not conscious of his parsimony and can therefore rationalize his tight-fisted behavior as frugality.

The dynamic theory of character does not, however, end at a point of illustrating conscious and unconscious character traits in order to explain a significant behavior. It inquires further as to the basic impulse or orientation that lies behind a specific character trait, which is also recognizable in other character traits. It presumes a character structure, and not only sees in someone's various character traits (or in many people's character traits) a random collection but rather seeks a common *orientation* of character that connects these diverse traits. This *character orientation*—namely that to which humans in the depths of their being desperately aspire—must be recognized if one wants to understand and change oneself or the behavior of others.

Usually, we can more easily recognize the *character orientation* of a person who has a stingy character *trait* that makes him so stingy when we take the person's other typical character traits into account. For example, we might observe a great passion for collecting that distinguishes itself by the way in which the person cannot part with anything, not even for the purpose of trading; he doesn't want to run any risk; his fearfulness shows itself perhaps in a mistrust of others who, of course, only want to take something away from him, or perhaps in a pronounced fear of loss. Giving away, bequeathing, donating are all things that he gladly leaves to others. Possessive pronouns accumulate in his speech; he tends to speak of *his* children, *his* treasured artworks, *his* needs and feelings.

What all of these character traits and behavioral problems share is a pleasure in wanting to possess and to hoard. Such a person has a hoarding character orientation, which gives his character traits a certain orientation and energy, and profoundly determines his behavior. The initial recognition of *character orientation* allows a deeper understanding of oneself, of another person, but also of a society or a social grouping whose thoughts, feelings, and actions are determined by (for example) a hoarding character orientation. In the Frommian art of living, a very central concern is the dependency of such character orientations on economic and social demands.

Character formations serve the psychological and sociobiological function for human beings of being a substitute for missing or diminished instincts. If man acts "according to his character, he acts quasi-automatically and consistently; and the energy with which his character traits are charged guarantees effective, consistent action beyond what the force of learning can accomplish" (*On My Psychoanalytic Approach*, 1990d [1969], p. 7).

In the first years of life, additional inner structural formations beyond biological and genetic tendencies must take hold, which then shape man's relatedness to himself and to reality.

From a psychological perspective, character formations are structurally vital constructions because they regulate relatedness to reality and interactions with oneself, with individual others, and with social groups. For Fromm, character is "the (*relatively permanent*) *form in which human energy is canalized in the process of assimilation and socialization*" (*Man for Himself*, 1947a, p. 59). It develops—as was already shown—primarily through experiences of the most diverse sort that are internalized, whereby experiences of relationship take on a special meaning.

Society within the individual—the social character

The theory of character that Fromm developed attempts to do justice to the fact that the impulses important for social coexistence have as great an impact on the character formation of the individual as his own very personal circumstances. Theoretically, then, a distinction must be made between the "individual character" and the "social character." The sociobiological function of character determines not only the formation of the individual character but also that of the *social character*.

> The social character constitutes the "matrix" or "nucleus" of the character structure of most members of a group. This character

structure develops as a result of the basic experiences and mode of life common to that group. (. . .) The development of the social character is necessary for the functioning of a given society, and the survival of society is a biological necessity for the survival of man.

On My Psychoanalytic Approach, 1990d [1969], p. 8

The separation of character theory from Freudian drive theory allowed Fromm not only a new view of personal character formation, but also a new understanding of sociopsychological phenomena: "If the energy of most people in a given society is canalized in the same direction, their motivations are the same, and furthermore, they are receptive to the same ideas and ideals" (*Beyond the Chains of Illusion*, 1962a, p. 77).

Social character takes on an important, socially stabilizing function, as its purpose is "to shape the energies of the members of society in such a way that their behavior is not a matter of conscious decision as to whether or not to follow the social pattern (. . .) and at the same time finding gratification in acting according to the requirements of the culture" (p. 79).

A member of a feudal society, for example, would have to develop a social character orientation that

enabled him to rule others, to harden his heart toward their misery. The bourgeois class of the nineteenth century had to develop an anal character which was determined by the wish to save and to hoard and not to spend. In the twentieth century the same class developed a character which made saving only a minor virtue, if not a vice, when compared with the trait of the modern character to spend and to consume.

Greatness and Limitations of Freud's Thought, 1979a, p. 62

Although already formed in childhood, the social character orientation is thoroughly subject to change, depending on the adaptive capacities of character formation to economic and social demands. The stabilizing function of social character therefore always also depends on how many people are capable of new character formations, when, for example, economic globalization and the push for modernization bring with them changes in socio-economic demands. If people cannot adapt their characters, the social character becomes "an element of disintegration instead of stabilization, as dynamite instead of a social mortar, as it were" (*Psychoanalytic Characterology and Its Application to the Understanding of Culture*, 1949c, p. 6).

Every society determines which thoughts and feelings reach an individual's consciousness and which must remain unconscious. "Just as there is a social character, there is also a *social unconscious*" (*Beyond the Chains of Illusion*, 1962a, p. 88). Fromm designates the social unconscious as

> those areas of repression, which are common to most members of a society; these commonly repressed elements are those contents, which a given society cannot permit its members to be aware of if the society with its specific contradictions is to operate successfully. The *individual unconscious* (. . .) refers to those contents, which an individual represses for reasons of individual circumstances peculiar to his personal life situation.
>
> p. 88

Various "socially conditioned filters" play a role in what must remain unconscious in a society. In addition to language and logic, those taboos defined by the dominant social character decide whether a need, wish, affect, unease or conflict, a sensation, stirring, fantasy, idea or perception may become conscious or must remain unconscious. (See *Psychoanalysis and Zen Buddhism*, 1960a, pp. 99–104; and *Beyond the Chains of Illusion*, 1962a, pp. 115–125.)

Let us return once again to the example of the abusive father whose well-rationalized sadism stems from an authoritarian social character orientation that served as a stabilizing function for authoritarian economic and political structures. What happens to the sadistic character trait when the requirements of the economy and socialization change to such a degree that violent rule and self-sacrificing submission no longer guarantee society's functioning? Undoubtedly, the corresponding sadistic impulse of the individual also diminishes in strength, meaning, and plausibility. Other character traits emerge and take on more weight, for example the impulse to participate, the desire for equality, fairness, and teamwork, but also the tendency toward unreliability, lack of interest, impermanence, indifference, etc.

Along with the fading of the sadistic character trait, the repression of the sadistic impulse also loses strength and thereby comes to be seen as a cruel and guilt-laden failure. Increasingly, defensive strategies help modify the manner in which it is lived out. One then fights authoritarian conditions and the exercise of power with powerful words, one speaks only in angelic tones or turns against oneself sadistically and is able to control oneself successfully. All of these, however, are only transitional phenomena that can be observed with changes in the dominance of certain social character orientations.

To summarize: In contrast to Freud, who traced conscious and unconscious emotional forces that regulate relatedness to the self and others to a particularly *instinctual* nature of man, Fromm showed that emotional forces always arise from the necessity to be *related* to reality. They develop their specifically human stamp in part based on innate affects, but in part they are formed only in the process of socialization. This means that many impulses and emotional forces through which we relate to ourselves and others are socially shaped. They can be found in their corresponding character formations. Such socially generated character orientations emerge from the needs and demands that an economy, society, and culture require for cohesion and stability.

The entirety of Fromm's scholarly thought was led by an interest to discover the socially shaped character orientation within each individual. And yet, it would be a complete misunderstanding to conclude from this that Fromm was only concerned with the socially well-adjusted person. On the contrary! Exploring social character orientations and their psychodynamics allowed Fromm to identify more precisely what a particular economy and society need for their own realization. At the same time, Fromm had a very good idea of what allows man to actualize himself. Ideally, the social character orientation would contribute to both society's and man's well-being. In this case, Fromm speaks of a "productive" or "biophilic" social character orientation, or a "being" oriented character.

In the next chapter, I discuss what, according to Fromm, allows man to actualize himself. Only then can we ask if the currently prevailing social character orientations help or hinder the realization of man. To ask what allows man to flourish, we must first return to look at the life of Fromm.

Figure 4 Fromm at Bennington, 1947, by Henny Fromm.
© Lit Fromm Estate.

3

How Man Succeeds

Love in the life of Erich Fromm

Given that for Fromm the practice of reason and love is the embodiment of a successful life, we should first ask what meaning love had in his own life. The capacity to love did not come easily to the author of *The Art of Loving*. On the contrary, until well into middle age, what Fromm wrote in this book also applied to him: "There is hardly any activity, any enterprise, which is started with such tremendous hopes and expectations, and yet, which fails so regularly, as love" (*The Art of Loving*, 1956a, p. 5). There are many reasons—both very personal as well as social—why one's own capacity to love may be limited or even destined to fail. Of particular significance for every person is the art of love that their mother and father modeled. This can either give wings to developing a capacity to love or cripple it. Let us turn our attention then to the maternal and paternal love that marked Fromm's childhood and youth. (For biographical details, see Funk, 1983 and 2000; Hardeck, 2005; Friedman, 2013.)

Fromm's father, Napthali, was thirty years old at the time of Erich's birth. By profession, he was a berry wine merchant, and not a Jewish theologian like many of his ancestors. With a tendency to anxiety and strongly attached to his small family, he suffered from feelings of inferiority because of his profession. He pinned all his hopes on his son continuing the line of Talmudic scholars. His love for Erich was a mixture of *tender attention* (as photos that show the twelve- and thirteen-year-old Erich sitting on his father's lap indicate), *anxious solicitude* (in winter, Erich was often not allowed to leave the house because he could catch a cold outside), and a very *ambivalent idealization*. When the gifted student took his oral exams as part of the dissertation proceedings at the University of Heidelberg, his father was convinced that his son would fail the test and then kill himself.

Fromm's mother was twenty-four years old when he was born. She came from a less religious home than his father and was seen by her relatives as a cheerful, sociable woman who set the tone for her family (he himself would later see her differently). Here, too, photos reveal more than Fromm's sparse statements about the sort of love this mother showed her son. (On the photos, see my Erich Fromm illustrated biography—Funk, 2000; on the question of love in the life of Fromm, see the more detailed Funk, 2006.) For example, we see a photo of mother and son in a park at the edge of a lake. With her right hand, the mother grasps the shoulder of the ten-year-old boy and presses him to her chest. At the same time, she props her left arm on her hip in a victory pose. Here, a very vigorous and *clutching mother love* becomes visible, which did not make it easy for the son—the only child, at that—to separate.

Another family photo shows how much the mother admired her son. Erich is around seventeen years old and as tall as his father. Just like his father, the son holds a walking stick in his hand and a hat—attributes of the bourgeois man of the era. The father looks into the camera, the son's eyes stray into the distance. Between the two of them, however, stands the mother. With her right arm locked in her son's, she directs her gaze—simultaneously full of expectation and admiration—to his face. As Fromm himself later admitted, his mother wanted him to become a great artist and scientist, a second Paderewski. At the time, Paderewski was a celebrated composer, pianist, and Polish politician who even served in 1919 for a short time as prime minister.

No one comes away unscathed by a narcissistic valorization, not even Fromm. Such valorization is linked to an admiring environment, which does not allow for an autonomous sense of self-worth, independent of others. Indeed, Fromm struggled long and hard to free himself from this enveloping and idealizing mother love.

Even if a young person's capacity to love is generally shaped by the love that his mother and father model, parents alone do not determine the development of this capacity. The striving toward independence and autonomy, as well as one's own independent desire to love, also influences all psychic development from the moment of birth onward. As one becomes an adult, this striving expresses itself in the search for people who make other experiences of love possible. Depending how debilitating or disturbing the parents' love may have been for a child's development, the search for new and alternative experiences of love may lead one back to relationships in which familiar patterns of parental attachment resurface.

Often, one must live through a whole series of disastrous love relationships before one is ready to forego unconsciously encountering in one's partner a parental love that keeps one in an infantile and dependent state. This belated process of cutting the cord of maternal and paternal love generally entails painful experiences of renunciation and loss. With all of the disappointment and suffering that goes along with the relinquishment of parental ties, what matters most is whether the desire to be able to love oneself persists. Because, as Fromm says elsewhere: "To choose to solve a problem by love requires the courage to stand frustration, to remain patient in spite of setbacks" (*Do We Still Love Life?*, 1967e). Such an unwavering desire to be able to love can be traced well into the middle of Fromm's life, despite several failed relationships.

Fromm overcame relatively easily the *paternal love* that limited his own capacity to love. Already as an adolescent he had found another, religiously trained, father figure in Rabbi Nehemia Nobel from the Frankfurt Synagogue on Börneplatz. Nobel offered in certain ways an alternative to Fromm's overanxious father. In his anxiety and feelings of inferiority, the father reflected social character traits that were typical for a majority of Jews at the time. But Nobel was a self-confident speaker and Zionist who for a short time also influenced Fromm to join a Zionist youth organization. We have already touched on another father figure who was even more impressive in his ability to live completely autonomously, namely Salman Baruch Rabinkow in Heidelberg. Rabinkow and Freudian psychoanalysis opened up a pathway for Fromm to discover his own autonomy, capacity for reason, and creative scholarly abilities.

Fromm's attempts to separate himself from an adoring maternal love were both more protracted and more painful. Without a doubt, a therapeutic transference love formed the backdrop for his 1926 marriage to Frieda Reichmann, eleven years his senior, and he hoped to find in Frieda another mother who would admire him. But a tuberculosis infection in 1931 ensured that he would need to be physically separated from Frieda.

While still in Davos, he got to know the psychoanalyst Karen Horney, fifteen years his senior. After his emigration to New York in 1934, their acquaintance developed into a relationship, one which never led to marriage but which certainly went far beyond their shared professional interests. Whenever Fromm left from New York to travel, Horney traveled with him. Both promoted a revised understanding of psychoanalysis. Horney, however, was an ambitious partner and the relationship was never completely free of rivalry. The liaison with Karen Horney lasted until 1943 and ended in a fierce argument, which also led to a division in the psychoanalytic institute that they had run together.

Some time after his break with Horney, Fromm met Henny Gurland, a woman his own age. Having fled the Nazis with Walter Benjamin from France, she experienced how Benjamin took his life at the Spanish border. In 1944, Fromm married this German-born newspaper photographer. Finally, Fromm appeared to have found the woman of his life. Together, in 1947, they built their own house in Bennington, Vermont.

No sooner had they moved into their new house when Henny became bedridden with a mysterious illness. Initially lead poisoning was suspected, then an extremely painful arthritic disease was diagnosed. Fromm canceled all commitments in order to care for Henny and keep her company. Out of love, he moved to Mexico with her in 1950. The climate there was supposed to help lessen the pain of the now opioid-dependent woman.

Fromm built a new life in Mexico City. In 1951, he began to train a group of physicians to become psychoanalysts and was appointed to a permanent professorship at the university. However, Henny's illness thwarted any intention Fromm had of keeping up with his teaching commitments and lecture invitations in the United States. He could not take her with him and he did not want to leave her alone. Fromm did everything for her, orienting his life entirely around her care, although this did not help lessen her suffering. The situation became unbearable. In June 1952, he found Henny dead in their bathroom.

Fromm was at an end with his attempts at love. He felt only failure, powerlessness, and abandonment. It was a terribly agonizing and strenuous way to separate himself from a self-image that was oriented toward an adoring maternal love and that led him to a solicitude that ensnared him in Henny's illness of addiction. Henny's death forced him to accept his own limitations, even his own failings.

Months later, Fromm again found the courage to begin a new relationship. For the first time, he became involved with an American, Annis Freeman from Philadelphia. Annis was a widow; she had suffered the death of three husbands. She had lived with her last husband in India, but after his death she returned to the United States. This woman was different from all the others with whom Fromm had been involved up until now. Annis was very attractive, sensual, and without professional ambition, but nevertheless a worthy partner in conversation. Fromm fell in love with her and they married in December 1953. She moved to Mexico to live with him. They built a house in Cuernavaca according to their own plans, where they lived from 1956 to 1973. Annis accompanied him on his month-long stays in the United States and later in Europe, and she supported his engagement in United States politics, with the disarmament and peace movements.

In his helpless parting from Henny and his love for Annis, Fromm had found that capacity to love which was free of childhood fixations and allowed for a direct encounter. Only now could the practice of his capacity to love truly align with his theory of love, and only now could he write the book *The Art of Loving*, which came out in 1956. What he now wrote in this book was also true for him: "Even whether there is harmony or conflict, joy or sadness, is secondary to the fundamental fact that two people experience themselves from the essence of their existence, that they are one with each other by being one with themselves, rather than by fleeing from themselves" (*The Art of Loving*, 1956a, p. 93).

What is good for man

The question of what allows man *to thrive* is, for Fromm, closely linked with the question of what is *good* for man. That someone is successful or has come into money and power is not an indication that such achievements will also benefit the person's mental well-being and the common good.

For example, there are those with character traits—such as obsessive people—who believe that they live well enough with a particular character orientation, although their psychic potential is massively impaired because they must always "play it safe" and use compulsive actions to fight against an existentially threatening anxiety. There are also social character orientations that allow a person to be extraordinarily successful professionally or politically, but lead him to become ever more depressed and lifeless or even "burn out." Neither the subjective feeling of a successful life nor social success can therefore serve as measures in themselves. Is it even possible to find a common standard for what is *good* for man and that therefore lets him *succeed*?

According to Fromm, it is possible. To anticipate his conclusion: From a psychological perspective, the measure of what is good for man, what furthers his as well as the public's psychological well-being, is *the preservation of his psychic capacity to grow*. (This ability underlies and exemplifies the concepts of "productive orientation," "biophilia," and the "being mode of existence.")

To find and substantiate the measure of the capacity for psychic growth, however, we must probe on a more fundamental level, taking stock of man's situation prior to and independent of the way in which he has been shaped by particular social demands. We must inquire as to man's existential conditions and, in the process, include those specifically human needs that—despite many similarities—differentiate him from animals.

The measure can then be found in that which allows man himself (and not a particular society) to grow or regress in the process of satisfying his existential needs. In Fromm's words, "The criterion of mental health is not one of individual adjustment to a given social order, but a universal one, valid for all men, of giving a satisfactory answer to the problem of human existence" (*The Sane Society*, 1955a, p. 14). Fromm uses the concept of human existence, by which he means that all people must not only satisfy certain physiological needs (like eating, drinking, and sleeping), but also always particular, uniquely human, psychic needs. Because they rank as an existential necessity for human beings, Fromm referred to them as "existential needs." According to Fromm, these include the need for relatedness, the need for rootedness, the need for a sense of identity, the need for transcendence, and the need for a frame of orientation and an object of devotion. These needs must always be satisfied, by each human being in every culture. Toward this end, numerous opportunities for satisfaction are available to man. (See *The Sane Society*, 1955a, pp. 27–66, and *The Anatomy of Human Destructiveness*, 1973a, pp. 230–242.)

These various existential needs reveal little about how they are to be satisfied. But, psychologically speaking, they do make clear that man has no choice but to be related to reality, to himself, and to others; that he must experience himself as belonging to a social group; that he must develop a value system and a vision of who he is, of who he would and would not like to be; that he feels an imperative need to want to overcome his immediate state and exert his own agency; it is also an existential need for man to pose questions of meaning, thereby creating a religious, spiritual, or philosophical frame of orientation and taking meaningful action.

These are all existential necessities that humans require to live, in other words, to thrive. Just as man's existence depends upon physiological necessities, such as nourishment, sleep, or reproduction, so, too, are there psychic necessities that imperiously demand satisfaction, because man is not otherwise endowed than with these psychic needs. (Fromm's theory of existential psychic needs thus represents his "drive theory"; it clearly distinguishes itself from Freud's various drive theories in that it does not anchor human biology in an instinctual constitution, but rather in man's neurobiologically determined need and capacity to shape his relatedness to the world and himself.)

The fact that all humans must satisfy these psychic needs, in order for the individual and society to *succeed*, does not answer the question of *how* they must be satisfied. Only the question about *how* can point us toward what is *good* for man, because we find therein "a satisfactory answer to the problem of human existence" (*The Sane Society*, 1955a, p. 1). The range of possibilities is enormous. For example, completely different answers are possible to the question of relatedness: relatedness may be aggressive, contemptuous, rivalrous, or appreciative, loving, caring or maternal, possessive, abusive, etc. Each of these ways of relating is possible, yet each has a different *effect* on man's psychic ability to grow and his mental health.

The essential question is therefore: What sorts of satisfaction of needs support the ability to grow and mental health, and what sorts hinder them? Asking the question in this manner, however, only makes sense under the assumption that there is something within man that makes the promotion of mental health desirable and that makes him want to avoid anything that hinders it. Can we identify in man a "predisposition" that generally inclines him to put into practice what is good for him and thereby furthers his mental health?

The primary tendency to grow

Even before neurobiologists discovered mirror neurons, identifying in the brain the "principle of humanity" and the capacity for empathy (see for example Bauer, 2005, 2006, 2008; Hüther, 1999), and long before infant research could show that humans already at birth are capable of being *actively* related to their environment (see for example Dornes, 1993 and 2006), Fromm was speaking of an inner primary tendency of all life, including human life, to develop and unfold its own powers of growth.

The inner primary tendency is an intrinsic potential common to all living things, namely to bring *one's own potential for growth into a state of development and integration,* and where possible to ward off opposing forces. "The primary potentiality develops if the appropriate conditions for life are present, just as a seed grows only if the proper conditions of moisture, temperature, etc., are given" (*The Heart of Man*, 1964a, p. 51). In contrast to Freud and his theory about the shared origin of the life and death drives, Fromm links "primary" with the idea that only the obstruction or frustration of the inner primary tendency allows the "secondary" potential to emerge. This secondary potential takes shape when the primary tendency is overwhelmed by competing external influences and social demands or by traumatic life circumstances that force people to satisfy their psychic needs in a way that makes them mentally ill.

A comparison with the body and a physical wound can be very helpful here: if unhindered, the body grows and develops according to its inner potential. If the body is injured, however, further physical development will depend on the degree of injury. There are injuries that heal without a trace; others leave behind scars and disfigurement; very serious injuries, however, can so deeply damage the dynamics of immunity and recovery that negative reactions and secondary diseases develop.

A similar dynamic exists in the psychic realm, only here the possibilities of injuring and disturbing the primary tendency are much more manifold and frequent, and there is a much greater dependency on the formative environment and its outlets for satisfying psychic needs. When man lives under conditions that "are contrary to (...) the basic requirements for human growth and sanity, he cannot help reacting" (*The Sane Society*, 1955a, p. 19).

Such reactions can be attempts to protect and reassert the primary tendency. Fromm speaks of a "humanistic conscience" (*Man for Himself*, 1947a, pp. 158–172) as a "re-action of ourselves to ourselves," which calls us back "to become what we potentially are" (p. 159). The reactions can also contribute, however, to a strengthening of the secondary tendency and lead to apathy, a loss of initiative, hate, and destructiveness, or to regressions and arrests at earlier developmental stages. In whatever ways the secondary tendency manifests itself, for Fromm it is always the consequence of an unrealized, because impeded or thwarted, primary tendency.

Reactions to the thwarting of the primary tendency toward growth and wholeness, such as those forces within man tending toward dependency, destruction, or selfishness, have far-reaching consequences for how we handle these reactions. If "destructiveness [is a] necessary consequence of failure to grow" (*To Have Or to Be?* 1976a, p. 172) and "the degree of destructiveness is proportionate to the degree to which the unfolding of a person's capacities is blocked" (*Man for Himself*, 1947a, p. 216), then destructive behavior cannot be overcome by forbidding it, repressing it, or defending against it. Rather, it must be starved at its source by dismantling the external and internal barriers that prevent the unfolding of human potential.

Let us inquire more closely about how to understand what primary tendency means, *how to bring one's own potential for growth into a state of development and integration.* Every living being strives primarily toward growth and the integration of his specific possibilities. But what does this mean for man in light of his existential needs?

The growth orientation of one's own powers

With the help of powers that do not belong to him, man has the potential to shape his life, and therefore satisfy his physical, intellectual, and emotional needs through external sources. Instead of going by foot, he can drive a car; instead of thinking on his own, he can seek out an advisor for help. Instead of using his hands to craft things, he can buy what he wants; instead of taking responsibility for shaping his own life, he can orient himself to parental expectations or find meaning in our entertainment culture; instead of actually loving, he can want to be loved. But, man also has the potential to make use of his own powers. When he does this, he observes that they increase and become stronger, that is, they grow. In contrast, if he makes use of external powers to lead a fulfilling life, he then experiences how these powers are expended.

And at the same time, he senses that making use of powers not his own allows the latter to diminish in strength.

Intrinsic growth-oriented powers can be of a mental, psychological, or bodily nature. One's mental power may be, for example, the ability to remember or to think or to imagine. Psychological powers can include the ability to trust, to be tender, to concentrate, to show interest, to love. One's physical power might be the ability to move, or muscular strength.

While one's bodily powers develop essentially on their own through physical growth and daily life, man's psychological, mental, and spiritual potential require an activating stimulation for their unfolding, that is, to allow the intrinsic power to emerge and ultimately be made available for use. Neurobiological studies and observational infant research likewise support the assumption that psychic, mental, and spiritual powers already exhibit spontaneous activity when infants are held, recognized, carried, satisfied, and mirrored by their maternal caregiver, in other words when they can express themselves in an affirming and emotionally holding attachment (see Peter Fonagy's concept of "mentalization"; Fonagy *et al.*, 2003).

Even though one's own psychological, mental, and spiritual powers differ from physical powers in their preconditions for emergence, all of these have one thing in common: only to the extent to which they are used do they grow and remain available as one's own powers. We can see this most clearly with muscular strength: when someone has an arm or a leg in a cast for several weeks and can no longer exercise his muscles, his physical power diminishes and must be slowly, and usually painfully, relearned by moving and exercising the muscles, in other words, by making use of this bodily power.

The same is true of one's own mental powers. For example, those who do not exercise and use their memory, but rather write down everything that they need to remember, will be able to retain less and less. And those who no longer make use of their capacity to imagine become even more unimaginative—as when, instead of training their power of imagination by reading a book, they prefer to view a film, thereby reducing to one predefined visualization the multiple avenues of fantasy that a book offers.

The same is true for all of our own psychic powers, which only grow and are made accessible to the extent that they are used. The capacity to love does not depend on being loved, but rather on one's own practice of loving: only those who are able to take a step toward another person and grow beyond themselves emotionally are capable of love. Only those who have confidence in others and can place their faith in someone or something else develop their capacity to trust. And only those who trust themselves to be caring and practice an intimacy without ulterior motives *are* caring, that is, tenderness becomes a characteristic or individual trait. Those who would like to stand on their own two feet and live their life autonomously will only be able to do so when they can take steps in the direction of independence and actually practice autonomy.

If the primary tendency is to take hold, the specifically intrinsic human powers, in other words, the mental and psychological potential for growth, must be put into practice. Only in this way can their quality of stimulating growth unfold as well as contribute to a higher and more differentiated development of human promise.

Conceptual approaches

Over the course of his life, Fromm made various attempts to conceptualize the singularity of growth-oriented human powers, that is, to see the psychic capacity for growth as a deciding criterion of what is good for man (for a more in-depth discussion, see Funk, 2003).

We find initial attempts in his book *Escape from Freedom* (1941a). Here, the concept of spontaneity served to qualify one's own powers as forces of growth for the self. Everything that happens of one's own accord (*sua sponte*) allows one to surmount external influence. The primary tendency expresses itself in "*spontaneous activity*," as activity stemming from one's own initiative. "For the self is as strong as it is active" (p. 260).

Six years later, in *Man for Himself*, Fromm introduced a concept central for his work, namely the "*productive character orientation*," defining it thus: "Productiveness is man's realization of the potentialities characteristic of him, the use of his powers" (*Man for Himself*, 1947a, p. 87). Fromm understood the concept of being "productive" in terms of its Latin origins (*pro-ducere*) as that which "leads man forth," by his own, specifically human powers. With regard to the three most important human possibilities of expression, he defined the intrinsic productive powers as "reason" (productive thinking), "love" (productive feeling), and "creativity" (productive acting). Fromm preferred to speak simply of the intrinsic powers of "reason and love."

In connection with his discussion of man's existential needs, which must always be satisfied, even if in the most diverse of ways, Fromm defined productiveness as *mental health* and *optimal development*:

> Mental health is characterized by the ability to love and to create (need for relatedness), by the emergence from incestuous ties to clan and soil (need for rootedness), by a sense of identity based on one's experience of self as the subject and agent of one's powers (need for a sense of identity), by the grasp of reality inside and outside of ourselves, that is, by the development of objectivity and reason (need for a frame of orientation and an object of devotion).
>
> *The Sane Society*, 1955a, p. 69

The question of growth and decay moved anew into the center of Fromm's focus when, in his 1964 book *The Heart of Man*, he distinguished between a "syndrome of growth" and a "syndrome of decay," and he characterized one's own growth-oriented powers as a *biophilic orientation* or *biophilia* (in contrast to necrophilia).

> Unification and integrated growth are characteristic of all life processes, not only as far as cells are concerned, but also with regard to feeling and thinking. (...) The person who fully loves life is attracted by the process of life and growth in all spheres.
>
> *The Heart of Man*, 1964a, pp. 46–47

The concept of biophilia signals a striking change in Fromm's thinking: the strong anthropocentrism in Fromm's previous thought now expands to include the (evolutionary) dimension of life itself, so that the question of what is *good* for man now refers to the capacity for growth inherent in all living beings. The love for that which is alive (biophilia) as a psychic capacity for growth is rooted in the primary tendency of all living things to want to grow and develop (see Funk, 2017).

In his late work *To Have Or to Be?*, Fromm ultimately defines productivity as *being mode of existence*, whereby he understands "being" to mean what the practice of one's own powers can bring forth from within. "We human beings have an inherent and deeply rooted desire *to be*: to express our faculties, to be active, to be related to others, to escape the prison cell of selfishness" (*To Have Or to Be?*, 1976a, p. 100). The most essential feature of the being orientation

> is that of being active, not in the sense of outward activity, of busyness, but of inner activity, the productive use of our human powers. To be active means to give expression to one's faculties, talents, to the wealth of human gifts with which—though in varying degrees—every human being is endowed.
>
> p. 88

The productive orientation

In light of the questions what is good for man and what allows him to succeed, Fromm coined and used different concepts, all of which, however, speak to the same experience, namely the capacity to draw from one's own growth-oriented powers by putting them into practice. Fromm clarified this psychic capacity for growth further in terms of thinking, feeling, and acting, and illustrated what he understood to be the character traits of *"productive reason"* (the capacity to use reason to perceive reality), *"productive love"* (the capacity for loving relatedness), and *"productive work"* (the capacity for the creative shaping of one's world). To explain in more detail:

1. *Productive work*: "In the realm of *action*, the productive orientation is expressed in productive work, the prototype of which is art and craftsmanship" (*The Sane Society*, 1955a, p. 32). Productive work has

nothing to do with activism and busyness, but rather "is characterized by the rhythmic change of activity and repose" (*Man for Himself*, 1947a, p. 107). If an activity is motivated and propelled by anxiety or irrational impulses, it does not meet the essential qualifications of productive work: such work must be done freely and of one's own accord (*sua sponte*). Even the simplest actions can offer possibilities for accomplishing productive work.

Just as the productive orientation of work cannot be measured by its outcome, so too is artistic quality an uncertain indicator for productivity. When the capacity for productive action joins forces with a talent for artistry or craftsmanship, very impressive examples of a productive orientation may emerge. The deciding factor for productive work, however, is the activation of one's growth-oriented powers and not its artistic quality (which today is increasingly dictated by the market).

2. *Productive love*: "In the realm of *feeling*, the productive orientation is expressed in love, which is the experience of union with another person, with all men, and with nature, under the condition of retaining one's sense of integrity and independence" (*The Sane Society*, 1955a, p. 32). Productive love also depends upon its being put into practice. If someone fantasizes about being in loving relation to another, but only lovingly approaches the other in his imagination, not much will happen. The capacity to love grows only in those who *are* loving and reach out to the other.

Regardless of whether the love is of a mother for her child, a love for humanity, an erotic love between two people, an altruistic love, or a form of self-love, productive love can be described more specifically by the following *characteristics*:

- *Caring* and a *feeling of responsibility* for the other: both indicate that "love is an activity and not a passion by which one is overcome, nor an affect which one is 'affected by'" (*Man for Himself*, 1947a, p. 98).
- *Respect* for the other and a *knowing understanding* of the other because without these features, caring and a feeling of

responsibility "deteriorate into domination and possessiveness" (p. 102).

- *Independence* and differentiation between two people who at the same time possess the capacity for an *unmediated* closeness with each other.

- A *correspondence between love of the other and of one's self.* "The attitude toward the 'stranger' is inseparable from the attitude toward oneself. As long as any fellow being is experienced as fundamentally different from myself, as long as he remains a stranger, I remain a stranger to myself too" (*Beyond the Chains of Illusion*, 1962a, pp. 171–172).

- The *wish to share* and to share of oneself, in other words, the capacity to give: "What matters is that which all men share, not that in which they differ" (*The Art of Being*, 1989a [1974–75], p. 84).

- An *interest* in everything and an openness for everything that is unknown.

- The capacity *to listen* and to be completely *present with another*, to be able to *empathize* with the other, his reality, distress, and joy.

- The capacity *to trust*. One does not learn to trust by first demanding that someone else deliver proof of his own trust; being able to trust is one aspect of love, and the ability becomes one's own to the extent that one acts in a trustworthy manner.

As with all characteristic *traits*, those associated with the productive orientation are still not sufficient indication of the existence of a productive *orientation*. The desire of someone who is driven by the wish to share can just as easily bespeak an authoritarian, even a narcissistic character orientation. Whether a productive orientation actually manifests itself in the desire to share can only be recognized by the life-enhancing or life-destroying effects that the practice of this character trait generates.

3. *Productive reason*: "In the realm of *thought*, the productive orientation is expressed in the proper grasp of the world by reason"

(*The Sane Society*, 1955a, p. 32). By "reason," Fromm not only means a capacity to understand things rationally and intellectually, but rather primarily the psychological capacity to be "reasonable," in other words, to be able to recognize reality without deformation or distortion, using all of one's sensual, cognitive, intellectual, and emotional abilities.

With his qualification of "undistorted," Fromm differentiates his understanding of reason from any subjectivist or intentionally wishful thinking. At the same time, his concept of reason has little in common with rationalism and instrumental reason. Reason here signifies neither knowledge nor expertise, nor an understanding of how something works, functions, or is put together.

Productive reason is much more of a mental capacity and indicates a particular mode, namely a "reasonable" mode of interacting with reality. This mode, too, must be practiced if it is to be accessed as a capacity that allows us to master our lives. It does not simply stand available to man as he develops his mind. Only he who attempts each time to see reality anew as it reveals itself to him—and not how he wishes, or perhaps would like to alter it, or how it is conveyed to him by special interest groups and the media—acquires the capacity to interact reasonably with reality.

In a media world that feeds on a performativity determined by desire and led by special interests, the capacity for a reasonable interaction with reality requires that people practice living their *own*, unmediated interactions with reality, form their *own* judgments, make their *own* observations, and take a critical stance toward any sort of mediated perception of reality (see Funk, 2012).

As with productive love, we can also describe productive reason by its more typical *characteristics*:

- While intelligence perceives things only in terms of their appearance, functioning, and use, the *capacity for reasonable interaction with reality* allows us "to penetrate through the surface and to grasp the essence of an object" (*Man for Himself*, 1947a, p. 97). "Reason involves a third dimension, that of depth, which reaches to the essence of things and processes" (p. 102).

- Productive reason manifests itself in the *capacity for objectivity and a sense of reality*, using man's full subjectivity. The capacity for objectivity means that "the subject is intensely interested in his object, and the more intimate this relation is, the more fruitful is his thinking" (p. 103).
- An additional characteristic is the *capacity for self-knowledge*; only he who is capable of making himself the object of knowledge and can see himself as he is can develop the capacity for objectivity.
- Productive reason is marked by an *authentic interest* in the object and simultaneously by *respect* for the object: "Objectivity does not mean detachment, it means respect" (p. 105).
- The capacity for a *holistic knowledge* is a further characteristic. Those who isolate a facet of the object and only wish to know this particular side, without a view to its wholeness, will never understand the particular facet correctly.
- Finally, productive reason is distinguished by a *capacity for concentration*. The capacity for an unmediated closeness in productive love corresponds to the *capacity for concentration* in productive thought (see *The Art of Being*, 1989a [1974–75], pp. 44–49).

The capacity for growth at the crossroads

When man tries to put his innate primary capacity for growth into action and to exercise his physical, mental, and intellectual powers of growth, these then become characteristics, or a productive and biophilic character orientation. He develops neural networks, or psychic structures, oriented around being that lead to an ever greater inner independence from outer and ego-alien forces (people, relational spaces, images of others). He is able to think, love, feel, fantasize, build, and act independently and through his own powers.

Unlike with Freud, for whom a passive infant with a "primary narcissism" stands at the beginning of human life, Fromm believes man comes into the world with the "primary tendency" to be related to reality through his own powers and actively establishes such a relationship with his intrinsic motor, sensory, and affective powers. With the development of further cognitive, emotional, and intellectual capacities, he is ultimately able to craft a pattern of his own growth-oriented powers that is "productively oriented."

From a psychological perspective, the fate of the child's primary capacity for growth depends in large part on the character orientations of its caregivers. If they live out their own intrinsic productive powers, then it would take some very traumatic situations or events to weaken the primary tendency or even to turn it into its opposite.

Fromm paid special attention not only to the growth potential within people, but also, and in the same way, to the individual's nonproductive powers, especially to those with a social origin. To stay with the example of child development: Fromm saw that selfish, anxious, possessive, clinging, dismissive, or codependent caregivers would hinder or thwart the primary tendency, which could result in the formation of a nonproductive character orientation.

What interested Fromm above all, however, was which nonproductive social character orientations exerted their influence on caregivers and if this influence and its strength could be modified through professional, economic, social, and political relations, as well as by cultural, familial, and religious constellations. For precisely this reason, Fromm directed his entire attention concurrently to social character orientations that stand in the service of society's success.

In our present moment, examining the destructive sides of society critically and urging social change meet with diverse sorts of denouncement: it is decried as pessimism, utopianism, presumptuousness, or romantic idealism. Only when the Third Reich and National Socialist society are the focus do a marked antipathy and critical stance become acceptable, and one finally dares to see the psychological effects of a "system." In the meantime, a marked antipathy to the 1960s has also taken hold, albeit for different reasons. This generation still dared to feel society's suffering and they therefore wanted to change society. Precisely this spirit is so unwelcome in our society, which wants to "think positive," feel upbeat, and be entertained.

The Frommian art of living is unthinkable without a critical approach to the dominant social character orientation and the economic, political, and social conditions that sustain it. This view has two points of origin: first, Fromm's psychoanalytic approach to people socialized in this manner; and second, the historically ever-present contradiction between what a society demands of character orientations for its own success and those different character orientations that man requires for his own well-being. The contradiction waxes or wanes according to how much of a productive orientation a society allows and encourages for its own success. Fromm's high sensitivity to this contradiction surely also relates to his own unmediated and painful experiences of the destructive effects that the Third Reich's character orientations required for its success, and to his studies on the authoritarian character.

For that reason, in the next chapter I explore the nonproductive social character orientation favored so strongly today and explore which intrinsic powers of growth are being thwarted—and perhaps now may be rediscovered and promoted.

This chapter, too, opens with a biographical segment. It begins with the destructive social character orientation of National Socialism and illustrates how Fromm found his way with it.

Figure 5 Fromm as a lecturer, 1960. © Lit Fromm Estate.

4

How Society Succeeds at the
Expense of Man

Erich Fromm's suffering in society

Although Fromm left the religion of his forefathers behind him, he never denied his Jewish origins and the way that Judaism shaped him. And from the perspective of an ascendant National Socialism, after joining Horkheimer's Marxist-oriented Institute for Social Research in Frankfurt, Fromm had a second flaw: he was a leftist intellectual. The members of the Institute were already aware of the threat that Nazi rule posed, as can be seen in their shift of the Institute's location as well as its financial reserves to Geneva, even before Hitler's seizure of power in January 1933. Because of his tuberculosis, from the summer of 1931 until his emigration to New York in May 1934, Fromm spent most of his time in Switzerland.

In emigrating, Fromm left behind almost everything that he had kept at his parents' house at 24 Liebigstraße in Frankfurt. He was allowed to take only a very few books and manuscripts, as well as some photos, upon emigrating from Switzerland. The Heidelberg "Therapeutikum" had already shut its doors in 1928. Fromm had gone to Berlin. The psychotherapeutic practice Fromm opened in Berlin at 1 Bayerischer Platz in 1930 closed again after his illness. In December 1933, his father died. Only after the pogroms in November 1938, in which synagogues were set on fire and Jewish businesses destroyed largely without interference, was Fromm's mother ready to leave Germany. With Erich's help, she fled first to London in 1939 and arrived in New York in 1941.

Like many other Jewish scholars who survived the Holocaust, Fromm never wrote anything about his personal experience of this time (see Fahrenberg, 2004, pp. 325–327). This may have to do with the fact that the paternal side of his family was small and in large part escaped the Holocaust. The situation was very different for his maternal side, that is, for the Krause family. Living mainly in Berlin, this side of the family was large and very close-knit (for more on the following, see Funk, 2005a).

Of the five of Rosa Fromm's sisters, two perished in the Holocaust. Her older sister, Sophie, was killed along with her husband, David Engländer, in Theresienstadt; her younger brother, Martin Krause, and his wife, Johanna, were deported east to the Trawniki camp and murdered there in 1942. His mother's oldest sister, Martha, and her husband, Bernhard Stein, managed to leave in 1939 to go to their children Fritz and Charlotte in Brazil (Charlotte was the cousin who loved to spend her childhood vacations with Erich in Frankfurt).

One of the mother's three cousins, Genja Krause, a daughter of the Talmudic scholar Ludwig Krause from Poznan, committed suicide in 1936 while in exile in Paris; another cousin, Gertrud Brandt, was "resettled" from Poznan to Ostrow-Lubelski, from there sent to a camp and murdered in 1943. Three of Gertrud Brandt's four children were persecuted. The oldest son and an avowed Communist, Heinz Brandt, spent the 1930s in Oranienburg prison and the period until the end of the war in the Dachau concentration camp. The second son, Richard Brandt, fled to Moscow and was murdered there in 1938. The third child of Gertrud Brandt, Lili Brandt, left for Moscow as early as 1932, where she became a doctor, returning to Germany only in 1984. The fourth child, Wolfgang Brandt, suffered from Down syndrome; he was deported to Ostrow-Lubelski and died there in 1942.

Erich Fromm's estate shows a series of papers that document the help he gave his relatives: he sponsored the emigration of Kurt Wertheim, a relative on his father's side; he supported his mother financially and made her emigration possible; he sent money to Gertrud Brandt in Ostrow-Lubelski; for his cousin Heinz Brandt he attempted everything—if in vain—after his prison release so that he might emigrate in the late fall of 1940 to Shanghai and from there to the USA;

in May 1941, Fromm signed—again, in vain—an "Affidavit of Support" for his uncle, Martin Krause, and Martin's wife, Johanna, to wrest them from the Holocaust. The letters of his maternal relatives always speak of Erich as their knight in shining armor in New York.

Fromm was well informed about what was happening in Germany, not only through his relatives but also through the critical American press, as his letters with Max Horkheimer in the 1930s indicate. Concern about political developments and fear about the fate of his family were always at the front of Fromm's mind.

Fromm knew of the powerlessness and defenselessness of Jewish people in Germany—they were stigmatized, denounced, and openly hated. He was aware that Jewish businesspeople could not hope to rely on insurance to cover the damage when their shops were destroyed by racist zealots, but would have to pay the expenses themselves; likewise, he knew that pogroms had declared Jews fair game, and that anyone could insult and abuse them with impunity; he was also aware that for his relatives the judiciary and the police no longer served any protective function against threatened or suffered injustices, but rather that they would be permanently hunted and humiliated like criminals. From the letters of his relatives (published in part in Funk, 2005a), who, after the start of the war, lost any chance to leave the "Reich," Fromm could piece together what it means to have to surrender all of one's possessions, to be banned from working, to be forbidden to enter any public institutions, to lose one's apartment, and finally to be picked up for "relocation"— that is, deportation.

Among the mementos that Fromm kept with his private documents was a copy of his beloved Aunt Sophie's final letter to her children and grandchildren in Chile before she and her husband David were deported to Theresienstadt and perished there. The letter bears the date of August 29, 1942, after the large-scale programs to exterminate the Jews had been decided upon.

> We will probably travel there [to Theresienstadt] soon, too, although we do not yet know the exact date. We are glad that we will meet each other there again. Father Br.'s friend, Dr. Alexander, is there, too.

Likewise, Aunt Flore and countless friends and acquaintances. Aunt Hulda will leave her apartment the day after tomorrow. It's apparently good there for us old people, especially the climate and the scenery. (...) Please just all stay healthy and don't worry about us. (...) Please greet all our loved ones, Aunt Martha, the Hirschfelds, the Steins, Aunt Rosinchen [Erich Fromm's mother], Erich, Altmanns, Meta, Ita and her husband, Greti, Aunt Irma and family. How nice it was that we were fortunate enough to know so many good and dear people in our life...
Published in Funk, 2000, p. 49

Developments in Germany made clear to Fromm how destructive a social character orientation can become, where a predominantly authoritarian character orientation left the majority of Germans primed not only to submit to megalomaniacal notions of power, war plans, and extermination programs, but also be inspired by them and back their *Führer*. Even now, the urgent question is how something like this could happen.

The Frommian concept of a social character offers an answer. Fromm's scholarly working through of his personal experiences of the Third Reich and his search for a sociopsychological explanation for the behavior of the masses is only *one* part of his attempt to come to terms with the past. This part finds its first literary expression in *Escape from Freedom* (1941a), in which Fromm applied his insights about sadomasochistic character (*Sozialpsychologischer Teil*, 1936a, GA I, pp. 141–187) to the authoritarianism and *Führer* cult of fascism and National Socialism.

At the beginning of the 1960s, Fromm gave a much broader answer in *The Heart of Man* with his concept of necrophilia—the characterological attraction to death and killing (see 1964a, pp. 37–46). Fromm then clarified this necrophilic character orientation in *The Anatomy of Human Destructiveness* (1973a) using the example of Hitler's personality and the many facets of the National Socialist regime's ideology, structure, and destructive practice. He also illustrated in a sociopsychological manner which segments of the German population felt themselves particularly attracted to sadism and necrophilia.

The *other* part of Fromm's attempt to come to terms with his experiences of the Third Reich was his political and socially critical commitment to a psychically "healthy" society, that is, to a society in which productive reason and love, biophilia and a being mode of existence, can become the dominant social character orientations.

Fromm put forward an initial outline in 1955 in his book *The Sane Society*. To aspire to a psychically healthy and reasonable society—a *sane society*—the economic, social, political, and cultural conditions that influence social character orientation must be shaped so that they have man's well-being as their goal.

In 1968, Fromm outlined a second concept in *The Revolution of Hope* (1968a), which emerged out of his intense involvement in the election campaign of the Democratic candidate for president, Eugene McCarthy. In his 1976 book *To Have Or to Be?* Fromm then added a third part with the title "The New Man and the New Society." Here, Fromm enumerated the multiple "difficulties the construction of the new society has to solve" with the following telling point: "It would have to solve the problem of how to continue the industrial mode of production without total centralization, i.e., without ending up in fascism of the old-fashioned type or, more likely, technological 'fascism with a smiling face'" (*To Have Or to Be?*, 1976a, p. 173).

Technological "fascism with a smiling face" appears to have now become reality. Fromm's sense of this as a contemporary threat illustrates a further aspect of his coming to terms with his experiences of the Third Reich and its destructiveness.

Fromm's past experience of destructiveness led him to focus his entire attention on a love for what is alive and on what is *good* for man and, for that reason, what allows *him to succeed*. In this way, he came to experience as well as conclude that such "destructiveness is the outcome of unlived life" and, for that reason, "the more life is realized, the less is the strength of destructiveness" (*Escape from Freedom*, 1941a, p. 182). Putting this insight about his experience of destructiveness into practice made Fromm extremely sensitive to all contemporary social developments that threatened to stifle the primary growth-oriented tendency.

Fromm's treatment of the Holocaust and the Third Reich touches on a central aspect of the art of living. As long as the focus remains exclusively on "never again" (fascism, Nazism, racism, the Holocaust), we continue an internal battle with a past destructiveness and cannot really free ourselves from it. Psychic energy becomes consumed in the fight against and the attempt to liberate from something, rather than being used for activating the psychic capacity for growth. If we put our own sensory, emotional, and intellectual powers into practice, they allow us to feel where life is thwarted *today* in our contemporary economy, culture, and society, and where new forms of destructiveness and violence emerge as consequences of unlived life. What Fromm said in 1966 in light of the Vietnam War applies just as well today to preventive wars such as Syria and even more to suicidal terrorist attacks: "There is only one hope to stop the wave of violence, and that is to become sensitive once more to all that is alive" (*The War in Vietnam and the Brutalization of Man*, 1990r [1966]).

The Third Reich, the Holocaust, current wars and terrorist attacks are all consequences of a *thwarting* of the primary tendency to grow for which it holds: "*if I cannot create life, I can destroy it*" (*The Sane Society*, 1955a, p. 37). If man is reduced to feeling only his lack of power to effect anything, his next best option is to thwart life itself by destroying himself and/or others. It is rare that social character orientations take on such a nonproductive dynamic that leads to a majority of the population as well as the forces of growth being blocked.

The social character orientations that Fromm identified and researched are distinguished by their non productivity, which generally—at least from a macrosocial perspective—does not lead to a thwarting and blocking but rather "only" to an *impediment* of the psychic capacity to grow. This, however, does not exclude these orientations from having an obstructive effect on individuals or on specially affected groups.

The following comments on several social character orientations attempt to show that, because particular economies and societies believe that they can only realize their own success at the expense of man, nonproductive social character orientations come to hinder certain psychic capacities for growth and the individual's own powers. In other words, they see their own well-being endangered by the practice of man's own powers.

To be sure, the use of one's own productive powers and the realization of the psychic capacity for growth represent the basic idea of an art of living as Fromm envisioned it. Without awareness of one's own nonproductive social character orientations and without a more productive interaction with the psychic potential for growth that they hinder, we cannot expect any real change. For this reason alone, a direct encounter with oneself and the other cannot avoid a confrontation with one's own nonproductive character orientations. In the following, with every orientation that I outline I ask which intrinsic powers must be revived and strengthened in order to reactivate the primary capacity for growth and allow it to become dominant.

The authoritarian character—at the expense of autonomy

Even though the authoritarian social character orientation is losing relevance in highly industrialized societies, it still plays a none too minor role in particularly privileged social groups such as the military, the law, medicine, in churches and (more or less fundamentalist) religious groups as well as of course on the right side (and in the meantime also the left) of the political spectrum.

Fromm speaks of an authoritarian orientation in business, politics, and society, but also in a psychological sense, as when relatedness to others, oneself, nature, work, etc. is marked by a (sadistic) exercise of *dominance* and by a (masochistic) exercise of *submissiveness*. Those dominating and those submitting are simultaneously and symbiotically linked to each other.

The *exercise of dominance* tends to appear in *interactions with others* in three separate and distinct ways (see *Escape from Freedom*, 1941a, pp. 142–143): either one wants to make and keep others dependent, using force to render them submissive, or to patronize them presumptuously and solicitously; or one wants to exploit and use others materially or emotionally; or one takes pleasure in making or seeing others suffer, hurting them, treating them cruelly, shaming or humiliating them.

Exercising dominance is also about *interacting with oneself*. Not others, but one's own body, affects and feelings, drives, sexual impulses, one's inner demons, etc., are to be dominated. Dominance is exercised here as self-control, which, when internalized, the authoritarian conscience recognizes; it then demands, rigidly and with relentless severity, discipline, deference, and obedience.

In the *acquisition of goods*, the sadistic side of the authoritarian character orientation reveals itself by an exploitative behavior that is untroubled by the claims and rights of others.

The *exercise of submissiveness* emerges *in interactions with others* through the idealization of those authorities who are supposed to lead, guide, protect, and provide as well as give directions and orders: the king is beyond reproach, the party is always right, the teacher is infallible, the theologian's God is omniscient, the theory is irrefutable. Submission to a strong or solicitous hand can be rationalized readily as love, loyalty, and gratitude.

In *interacting with oneself*, submission manifests as a renouncement of one's own claims, rights, and self-determination, one's own boundaries and individuality. It correlates with self-denial and selflessness, feelings of inferiority and worthlessness, a sense of guilt and a fear of punishment, impotence and deep feelings of powerlessness. More unconscious than conscious, the masochistic quality of submission can be also seen in those situations in which one feels small and weak, a failure, dogged by bad luck, in the wrong, or sabotaged by oneself.

In the *acquisition of goods*, submission shows itself in a receptive stance that wants to take in everything. The individual expects all that he longs for, hopes for, needs, and uses is his entitlement: an inheritance or gift, it will be given, presented, imparted, served to him.

In principle, the sadistic and the masochistic sides are equally present in authoritarian people, although a sense of identity is usually very one-sided with one aligning with only one side or the other. Frequently, both sides are dispersed among different roles. Someone submissive then lives out his sadistic side through rigid self-control. Or someone enacts his dominance on a submissive person, while at the same time behaving subserviently toward superiors, God, or fate, kowtowing to those above and browbeating those below.

The authoritarian social character orientation usually maintains its imprint through hierarchically organized power structures in the economy and society. In the political sphere, authoritarian structures were clearly recognizable in absolutism, the Prussian state, and in dictatorships such as the Third Reich or in those countries with "real existing socialism." The degree to which the current metastases of bureaucratization and management mania with their instruments of regulation—such as the often equally hierarchically organized business system of controlling—create a new authoritarianism is not easy to answer. Fromm correctly points out that the modern bureaucrat is less drawn to the exercise of dominance than to a quasi-mechanical, formalistic, and lifeless sort of interaction with himself and others, which is typical of the necrophilic character. "The modern bureaucrat has not become a suddenly lovable sadist, but rather he experiences himself as a thing, just as other people for him are also only things" (*The Anatomy of Human Destructiveness*, 1973a, GA VII, p. 267—see note).

The *psychic dynamic* of the authoritarian social character orientation can be described as follows: in response to the pressure that the dominant person exerts, the submissive individual discharges his own autonomous powers that allow him to be competent, knowledgeable, strong, independent, and free, and projects them onto the authority figure. *The authority* is now powerful, wise, magnificent, strong, solicitous, well-meaning, honorable, etc. By submitting to authority in order to connect with it symbiotically, the submissive person succeeds in partaking derivatively in his own powers which he has projected onto the authority.

Someone's actual sense of identity with an authoritarian orientation, generated by the projection of his own growth-oriented powers, must be repressed, and it can remain repressed as long as the submissive person remains secondarily connected to his own powers through his symbiosis with authority. If the mutual symbiotic dependence comes under serious threat, then the submissive person experiences feelings of powerlessness, inferiority, abandonment, helplessness, aloneness, shame, guilt, and worthlessness. "The more powerful an idol becomes—that is, the more I transfer on it—the poorer I become and the more I am dependent on it, since I am lost if I lose that onto which I have transferred everything that I have" (*Modern Man and the Future*, 1992d [1961], p. 24). The fact that the one exercising dominance is dependent upon someone submitting, without whom he cannot experience his own practice of domination, is based upon mutual symbiosis. He simultaneously projects his own incompetence and weakness onto the submissive person, leaving the latter to hold his unacceptable sense of identity.

The practice of dominance and submission is also evident in the following typical authoritarian *character traits*:

- The *demonstration of power and violence*, grandiosity, superiority, dominance, ostentation, willfulness, or high-mindedness.
- *Submission* to orders and commands of authority or circumstantial constraints, or in an *attitude of resignation* which patiently expects that everything good will flow from those in authority.
- *Pleasure in punishment* and torture, and the *admiration and idealization of authority*, that which is authoritarian, strong, and powerful (which is why values like honor, respect, and deference are of great importance).
- The demand for and the inclination to blind *obedience* as well as the ability to be faithful, humble, and grateful, as well as compliant.
- The desire simply to do one's *duty* (as a civil servant, worker, police officer, soldier, etc.) or, in religious and ethical contexts, the desire *to serve*.
- The *suppression of any critique* and the repression of any rebellious protest.

- The *love of law and order*, stricter regulations, harsher enforcement and *hostility toward anything autonomous*, defiant, oppositional, or anything that strives for independence.
- *Contempt for the weak* and helpless, and an *emphasis on social differences* and class antagonism.
- A *patronizing solicitude* (by a teacher, a nurse, a doctor, a mother, a church—all of which purport to know better what is good for any particular person) and in the *adherence to structures of dependency*.

More and more people today see authoritarian structures in society and politics, as well as their own authoritarian character traits, as belonging to the *past*, because they no longer offer any orientation for their current experience of self or community. People have not only participated in the transformation of the economy, society, politics, and culture, but they have also felt these changes in their own social character orientation. Such interior changes have also made possible a critical stance toward, if not a complete rejection of, those social models, economic philosophies, political systems, lived environments, and value systems that are clearly authoritarian.

What allowed an authoritarian society to succeed (if at the expense of man's own well-being) is precisely the way that the exercise of dominance and submission regulated, supported, and stabilized it. We can see this on all levels, whether the focus is the authoritarian distribution of power in the economy and society, or the authoritarian organizational structure of the state and its powers, or the authoritarian organization of labor with exploitative employers and compliant workers, or the authoritarian educational system, or the authoritarian organization of finance and management with its hierarchical administration, or the authoritarian criminal justice system that secures social coexistence, or a cultural life dominated by authorities.

The value system had to serve the authoritarian structure, which is why statutes and requirements were to be respected, while disobedience and opposition were punished. High-priority values included civility, dependability, conscientiousness, obedience, gratitude, loyalty, trust, subservience, humility, devotion, dedication, discipline, self-denial, sacrifice, honor, truth, etc. Such values are of course not without meaning for man's well-being today. However, they were practiced primarily because they contributed to the success of authoritarian society, and *not* because they served to help man thrive. Someone who heeds an external authoritarian order, or the call of his own authoritarian conscience, heeds an authority's commands. He does not follow his own psychic potential for growth and that which would allow him to flourish as a free and autonomous person.

With regard to the art of living, it is important to realize not only which social character orientations are operating within oneself. Even more important is gaining a sense of which primary tendencies and intrinsic powers are prevented from contributing to man's development and success by the predominant social character orientation. To strengthen the productive orientation, one's excluded or supplanted powers that had supported social well-being must be rediscovered and practiced.

We can see which intrinsic productive powers remain undeveloped by looking at how people suffer psychically and the ways in which they do not get along with themselves or their environment, because their inner psychic structures and forces of growth are weakened. This must be addressed individually with each relevant social character orientation.

In the authoritarian social character, underdevelopment of one's own powers related to the *autonomy of the individual* are most notable. Whether demonstrating their power or feeling powerless, authoritarian people always suffer from dependency and a lack of self-sufficiency. Not only is the submissive person nothing without authority, the sovereign is toppled from his throne when his subjects refuse him allegiance. Both can neither abide (nor allow) the development of any capacity to say no, to disobey, to defy—self-assertion, self-determination, and a self-confident aggression are forbidden. Instinctual and affective impulses that strengthen and help express identity and self-efficacy, self-reliance and self-worth, maturity and independence, are threatening. Should these impulses make themselves known, despite repression and disavowal, they elicit anxiety (about loss), irrational guilt feelings and fears of punishment. Authoritarian people would like to impede and obstruct anything that blazes an independent trail, be it sexual desires, affective perceptions, uncontrolled emotions, adolescent children, or spontaneous and undisciplined actions.

If the primary tendency for growth and a productive orientation is to be promoted by an authoritarian social character orientation, there is no alternative but to discover autonomy within those capacities now afflicted by anxiety and inhibition, and to begin to tolerate the feelings of anxiety and guilt that set in with this "counteraction" and with the dissolution of the symbiotic entanglement. Without some disobedience, an escape from authoritarian relations is inconceivable.

Much of what Fromm wrote about the productive orientation or a humanistic alternative relates primarily to the authoritarian character orientation. For that reason, his alternative models often refer to the authoritarian orientation. Yet, Fromm discovered and explored a range of other social character orientations in which different primary tendencies impede the success of society. They thus remain undeveloped and man's well-being is endangered.

The marketing orientation—at the expense of a sense of identity

The marketing orientation is all about marketability and sales strategy. Whether the focus is goods, services, art works, religion, pedagogical concepts, or one's own personality, actual use value—of a product, a theory, an offer to help, an achievement, perhaps in marketing one's own personality—is not decisive. Rather, what matters are exchange value and marketability. Of foremost importance is that one can *successfully sell* goods and oneself as if they were commodities, which will depend upon the marketing strategy.

Products as well as one's own personality are understood solely as commodities that need to be communicated well. Entire professions devoted to helping, caring, healing, advising, and managing now speak of customers, products, profitability, effectiveness, efficiency, and quality assurance, that is, they understand their actions and their services as commodities to be sold.

Marketing and sales strategies not only determine economic and social life; in order for a society to succeed, socio-economic demands must be internalized and lead to the social character of the *marketing orientation*. Here, dominance and submission do not determine hearts and minds; rather thoughts, feelings, and actions zealously orient themselves around questions of marketability and sales strategy, both in relation to products and in relation to the self.

Because all aspects of life revolve here foremost around marketing, the focus is always on the *visual appearance of the product* or of one's own person. Of course, content and utility cannot be completely neglected, but the successful sale really only begins when all interest turns to the product's staging—the packaging, appearance, image, glamour, its transmission, didactics, performance, representation, outfit.

The shift is especially noticeable when the focus is *the marketing of one's own self*. What someone in fact does and achieves, what abilities he actually has, who someone really is and how one experiences oneself— this all plays a secondary role at best. Much more important is how to represent one's alleged efforts, how to document one's skills training, soft skills, and unique qualities, how to make one's highly styled personality seem authentic, how to showcase a self-confident image. Job application training is a must if one still wants a fighting chance in the labor market.

The following important *character traits* should make clear the degree to which the marketing orientation determines our contemporary public and private life:

- Market-based behavior is reflected as an economic requirement in the psychic pursuit of *adaptation and conformity*—following the motto, "I am who you want me to be." What "everyone" does, reads, wears, buys, etc., becomes both important and right.

- A market-oriented economy requires extensive *flexibility*, not only to meet always changing demands, but especially to increase economic productivity by making production and work processes more flexible. This economic requirement is reflected in a corresponding character trait: the marketing character loves flexibility, variety, everything new and different, the indeterminate and impermanent, the challenge, playing with different personality roles.

- *Mobility*, too, as an economic requirement of a globalized economy returns in a characteristic desire to be on the move. The marketing character does not feel itself bound to any one place or strongly rooted, but rather can be everywhere and nowhere at home. An inability to be mobile any more is a very heavy blow for him.

- For the person focused on marketing, on the level of values and orientations everything turns on the question of what sells, of outcomes. In professional as well as personal life, therefore, the *pursuit of success* plays a very central role. Failure to succeed is a crushing verdict.

- In terms of relationships, the marketing-oriented person differs considerably from the authoritarian. Where the authoritarian seeks a firm emotional attachment and dependence, the marketing-oriented person pursues *detachment and impermanence*. Deeper ties (to an enterprise, to one's own self-image, to other people) are incompatible with flexibility and the pursuit of success. A relatedness that can always be put aside requires, on the one hand, a certain measure of distance and indifference, and on the other, tolerance and fairness.

- The pursuit of detachment in relationships corresponds to *the pursuit of de-emotionalization and coolness* on the level of feelings. Feelings are "sand in the gears," they disrupt productivity and are equated with irrationality. What counts is a clear head, cool intellect, the purely cerebral, psychological tricks and social engineering.

- While the *effort to objectify people* is also typical for the
  necrophilic social character orientation, this trait plays a
  significant role for the marketing orientation as well. The concept
  of *social engineering*, for example, already reveals this in that the
  engine—the machine—has the power. Humans are viewed as
  objects, and are measured like machines by their output and
  efficiency: Isn't it wonderful when someone thinks, produces, and
  functions as reliably as a machine? At the same time, *objects are
  humanized*, as when commodities are ascribed a personality, such
  as the bed in the furniture store named "Robert" or snack foods
  that produce a state of bliss.

Already in *Escape from Freedom* (1941a, pp. 185–206), Fromm had described "conformism" as a mechanism of escape through which people, out of a fear of freedom, "sacrifice" their uniqueness and individuality to adapt to the market. Six years later he then described the marketing orientation of character in depth (*Man for Himself*, 1947a, pp. 67–82). The marketing-oriented ideal is the chameleon that can effortlessly adapt its color to any environment and demand—nothing immutable hinders its successful survival.

Fromm uses as an illustration of the marketing orientation the figure of Ibsen's Peer Gynt, whose personality is like an onion:

> One layer after the other can be peeled off and there is no core to be
> found. Since man cannot live doubting his identity, he must, in the
> marketing orientation, find the conviction of identity not in reference
> to himself and his powers but in the opinion of others about him. His
> prestige, status, success, the fact that he is known to others as being a
> certain person are a substitute for the genuine feeling of identity.
>
> *Man for Himself*, 1947a, p. 73

The *psychodynamics of the marketing character* bear a certain relation to the authoritarian character. Both orient themselves toward an object. In the marketing orientation, however, this object is not an authoritarian person or institution, but rather the anonymous and constantly changing authority of the market. One cannot submit to this authority.

One also cannot build a stable emotional attachment to it. If someone wants to sell something or himself, he can only stay attuned to current market trends and align his products or his personality entirely according to market preferences.

This adaptation is even more successful the less one's individuality— individual and unique aspirations, wishes, feelings, interests, characteristics—is hampered in its chameleon-like adaptation to the wishes, interests, and expectations of the market. To stay with the chameleon comparison: a chameleon is special in that it is not identifiable by its color, but rather is always taking on the color of its environment. What is true of the chameleon with regard to skin color is true of the marketing character with regard to many identifying features. There is rarely anything constant and clearly identifiable that characterizes the marketing-oriented person as unmistakably unique. He wants to be what the market—the social environment and expectations—makes of him. By adapting to cultural patterns and expectations, "the individual ceases to be himself" (*Escape from Freedom*, 1941a, p. 184).

The marketing-oriented person wants to renounce anything that could distinguish his own unique, individual personality. His inherent nature becomes alien to him and he encounters it as a role and personality into which he slips so that he can be successful in the market. This, however, makes it impossible for him to sense his own identity as belonging to him and to experience his own individuality.

> In the marketing orientation man encounters his own powers as commodities alienated from him. He is not one with them but they are masked from him because what matters is not his self-realization in the process of using them but his success in the process of selling them. Both his powers and what they create become estranged, something different from himself, something for others to judge and to use; thus his feeling of identity (...) is constituted by the sum total of roles one can play: "*I am as you desire me.*"
>
> *Man for Himself*, 1947a, p. 72 ff.

Here is not the place to delineate how intensely our current economic and social system uses the marketing-oriented social character for its own success. Worth noting, however, would be the fact that the marketing orientation does not favor the use value of products but rather their exchange value and their suggested (currently more important than emotional) added values; the concentration of firms that dominate the market, the intensification of predatory competition, the liberalization of trade, the globalization of production and its stakeholders, the liberalization of financial markets, etc.

Without sophisticated and elaborate marketing strategies—one only need think of expenditures on advertising and publicity—the economic system would hardly survive. Every service, institution, organization, every club and every offer to help, must attract attention to itself, represent itself, be present in public, especially in social media and in the public sphere of the internet—the image must be cultivated and cared for. In the most personal areas of relationships and intimacy, the desire to be happy and well-liked by others defines attachment and self-experience. The ultimate feelings are not power and dominance, but rather success and winning. We have long since become a society of two classes: those who succeed in the market—the winners—confront those who fail—the losers.

According to social standards, those who are not or are no longer marketable belong to the losers—for whatever reasons, they cannot adapt and do not want to let themselves be marketed. With the art of living as Fromm understands it, however, society's well-being does not matter, but rather what *enables man's psychic well-being.* Let us examine which primary tendencies fall by the wayside with the marketing-oriented social character and which deficits in human productivity the marketing-oriented person demonstrates. Here, too, it is important to regain a sense of what is or has been lost when everything in life is measured by the marketability of work and personality. Only then is it possible to begin to re-exercise our own productive powers that have been and will continue to be impeded by socially generated aspirations within the self.

First, certain *behavioral problems* that the marketing-oriented person shows in interactions with others and himself should be mentioned, as they point to which inner psychic structures have been weakened. A very obvious *superficiality* of relationships led Fromm to use the concept of *alienation*, especially with regard to its clinical relevance, in illustrating the example of a marketing-oriented person. People are and remain strangers to each other, because relatedness to another is *based neither on any deeper feelings nor on any real interest in the other.* "When the individual self is neglected (. . .) not they themselves but interchangeable commodities are related. People are not able and cannot afford to be concerned with that which is unique and 'peculiar' in each other" (*Man for Himself*, 1947a, p. 74).

Intimate relationships are based on mutual *fair play*, in which each person must be acceptable to the other. The ability to love does not mean finding the other person attractive and lovable because of who he or she is; to be able to love now means understanding how to make oneself attractive for the other person in order to gain his or her affection (self-promotion demands continuous effort). Marketing-oriented people enjoy being *calculating*. Other people and their environment are rarely ever seen for who they are, but rather are used in an instrumentalized manner, in other words solely from the perspective of one's own success, benefit, and advantage. Relationships must pass the test of being "profitable"—for one's own success. These are the roots of the universally lamented *egotism* of the marketing-oriented person.

The problems in interpersonal behavior can all be psychologically linked with the deficits of the marketing-oriented person in relation to himself and his experience of himself (his sense of identity). Who a person truly is, what he really feels and thinks and wants, his authentic self-experience, his actual needs, aspirations and longings—this all feels alien and is not sensed as belonging to him, as psychodynamic observations have shown.

According to Fromm, the *need for a sense of identity* belongs to those essential human needs that must always be met. No one can remain mentally and emotionally healthy without a sense of "I" (see *The Sane Society*, 1955a, pp. 62–63). Even if this need for a sense of identity can be satisfied in various ways, only a productive satisfaction allows man to experience his individuality and gain a sense of who he is, separate from other people, collectives, or institutions.

Such a sense of identity and awareness of one's own individuality develops only when man can perceive the differences between his own thoughts and feelings as separate from others', and therefore can say "I" (which is why "I" is one of the last words a child learns to use when he wants to speak about himself). This self-awareness grows stronger to the degree that people practice perceiving their own thinking, feeling, and acting as their own, and are able to differentiate this from the thinking, feeling, and acting of other people.

But what does the marketing-oriented person do? He, too, satisfies his need for a sense of identity, but he makes the satisfaction of this need dependent upon his success in the marketplace. He can only sense himself when he makes it and is successful. Someone else decides about his sense of identity: his response, sales figures, quota, success, fans. If success deserts him, because his marketing strategies in the form of promotional personality traits (such as: always appearing friendly and obliging, interested and compassionate), professional competencies or a self-confident air no longer work or are no longer desired, he not only becomes a loser, he above all loses himself: he starts to falter, "crashes," becomes depressed and feels internally empty, without motivation and bored.

Of course, he attempts to skirt these dangers; it's no surprise that he cannot allow himself to become aware of his identity loss and instead, filled with pride and narcissistic valorization, sees himself as a unique individual. Still, he might notice in the many details of his daily behavior how dependent he is upon success and how little he can tolerate failing, not being appreciated by others, a more modest success quota, a rejection of his efforts, a cut in his bonus, the movement of his client base to the competition, the ingratitude of his children, etc. Such experiences threaten to make him lose his sense of self.

In reality, the marketing orientation corrupts his sense of identity and impedes the ability of his psychic capacity of growth to experience itself as identical with his self-experience and his own powers. Someone who lives under social conditions that generally lead to a loss of a sense of identity based on one's capacities and strengths can only *preserve or regain a productive orientation* by the purposeful exercise of those intrinsic powers that build identity.

The point is not to do the opposite and thereby be rigid instead of flexible, or refuse to perform instead of try to succeed, or withdraw from competition in order to escape the rat race. Those who deny the nonproductive impulse are still engaged with what is nonproductive, and are not yet exercising their productive powers.

Exercising one's own powers in the face of a nonproductive marketing orientation means making space again for *one's own powers that build identity.* It is not so farfetched to recall here the "battles" of two- to five-year-olds, or teenagers, who attempt to free themselves from their primary and familial ties, and want to validate their own will and independence, or their power, worldview, and ability to plan their own life—if need be, with conflict. More concrete examples include:

- the courage to feel one's own feelings, to think one's own thoughts, and to determine one's own actions;
- the mobilization and activation of one's own sensory gifts: listening exercises, visual exercises, touching exercises, movement exercises—in order to remember that we have eyes with which to see and ears with which to hear and skin that allows us to touch and feel;
- a tolerance for emotionality (one's own affects and feelings) that is not oriented around success;
- the support of all activities and expressions of life that can be realized independently of mechanical and technical means;
- the insistence on a space and time that belong only to oneself;
- the claim and use of a protected space outside of the market (such as musical activities and interactions with loved ones);
- the privileging of (process-oriented) activities that require commitment, interest, and emotional attachment regardless of outcome;

- the capacity to not meet expectations;
- the acceptance of disadvantages and the endurance of adversity;
- the refusal to prostitute oneself for marketing reasons;
- the acknowledgment of one's own limits and given limitations;
- the respect and regard for the capacities and limitations of others;
- the courage to see also the dark sides of life, to look squarely in the eye of a life that has failed or gone wrong;
- the practice of a productive consumption in which one is oriented only to the use value instead of the market and added value.

The narcissistic character—at the expense of interest in the other

A social character formation that has become more prominent in recent decades is the narcissistic character, both as an individual character (a classic example would be the personality of Donald Trump), and as a socially accepted and supported narcissism among the broader population, in other words as a social character.

> Narcissism is an orientation in which all one's interest and passion are directed to one's own person: one's body, mind, feelings, interests, and so forth. (...) For the narcissistic person, only he and what concerns him are fully real; what is outside, what concerns others, is real only in a superficial sense of perception; that is to say, it is real for one's senses and for one's intellect. But it is not real in a deeper sense, for one's feeling or understanding. He is, in fact, aware only of what is outside, inasmuch as it affects him. Hence, he has no love, no compassion, no rational, objective judgment. The narcissistic person has built an invisible wall around himself. He is everything, the world is nothing. Or rather: He is the world.
>
> *The Art of Being*, 1989a [1974–75], p. 117

The social acceptability of the narcissistic social character formation, along with an overemphasis on the individual, also appears to have led to narcissism being primarily understood as something completely normal. Even the professional literature posits that everyone needs a healthy sense of narcissism, even for biological reasons of survival. The argument continues, however, that this normal narcissism can become pathological, a disordered narcissism.

In order to avoid any definitional misunderstandings in the following remarks about Fromm's understanding of narcissism, I would like to point to the distinctions and differentiations that he made: Fromm's social-psychoanalytic approach implies that every person must necessarily be self-related. This relatedness to oneself, however, has nothing to do with narcissism. As with relatedness to other people, a relatedness to oneself can be satisfied in various ways: solicitously, negligently, harshly, mercilessly, lovingly, with interest, etc. Here too: everything is possible, but not every way of satisfying the need for a sense of identity encourages the psychic capacity for growth and allows man to thrive.

By the end of the 1930s, Fromm had already developed a psychology of the self and had posed the question about how a selfish or narcissistic way of relating to oneself can develop (*Selfishness and Self-Love*, 1939b). In the following years, he made a clear distinction between "self-love" and "self-interest" on the one hand, and "selfishness" on the other (*Man for Himself*, 1947a, pp. 119–140). This distinction forms the basis of the psychological insight that "the selfish person does not love himself too much but too little" (*The Art of Loving*, 1956a, p. 60). Fromm then expounded upon his insights on individual and social narcissism in *The Heart of Man* (1964a, pp. 62–94).

In contrast to what much of the psychoanalytic literature claims, for Fromm there is no normal or biological narcissism. Nor does it make any sense to speak, as Freud did, of a "primary narcissism" of the infant and toddler; but there is a growing capacity for love of and interest in the self. The dependency of the infant and toddler on an unconditionally loving, protective, nourishing, attentive, empathically mentalizing and mirroring caregiver has nothing to do with the needy child's narcissism and self-centeredness. (The fact that an infant can neither stand nor walk for a long time does not make him crippled in our eyes. Why, then, should we see an infant as a narcissist?)

The development of self-love and self-interest is part of a lengthy educational process in which—psychologically speaking—internalized representations of experiences of reality and other people (object experiences) begin to emerge. Depending on what sort of growth-inducing ("productive") quality these repeated experiences have, they lead to a more or less stable sense of trust in oneself and in the surrounding environment.

The existence of something like a self as a psychic and neural structural formation can be felt in the following simple observation. When we hear criticism or have doubts about ourselves, or in negative interactions with other people, we don't feel the ground slip out from under us, but rather we can more or less clearly sense the difference between their questioning and how we experience ourselves. The more productive and growth-oriented the quality of stable internalized representations of experiences are, the more self-love and self-interest can develop, and the less antagonistic experiences of our faith in our self and in others shake our sense of identity and self-esteem.

The opposite, however, is also true: the less our representations of experience in childhood, but also in adulthood, contribute to our sense of feeling accepted, wanted, valued, sought, affirmed, encouraged, perhaps because those surrounding us only find us burdensome, or in their own selfish or excessive expectations are only disappointed in us, the more fragile our internalized representations of experience are or will be. And the more dependent we are and will be on actual experiences of praise and recognition.

This state of reliance on affirmation and praise means a humiliating, because permanent, dependence. For many this becomes so unbearable that in their self-centered character formation they seek a lasting escape: *they make themselves independent of the recognition of others by imagining their own greatness.* The others, the girlfriend, the partner, the colleague, the children, the patients are only of interest when they serve one's own greatness, that is, when they serve a mirroring or complementary function. Any interest in others' selves or their difference, even their foreignness, gradually wanes, because all attention is focused solely on the self. For Fromm, therefore, narcissism is always something selfish. It results from a lack of self-love and self-interest.

Such an escape from an unbearable to a narcissistic experience of identity always contains a *distorted perception* of oneself, but also of reality outside of oneself. This sort of distorted perception can generally be described as *idealizing* or *devaluing*. For that reason, narcissistic people are most easily recognized by their concern with greatness and idealization, or worthlessness and devaluation.

The most familiar sort of narcissistic self-perception is *self-idealization*: someone experiences himself as grandiose, and imagines himself the best, greatest, purest, smartest, most perfect, and most successful. A narcissistic person may be conscious of this fantasy, openly living it out, or it may be unconscious, and he experiences himself as normal and modest—or he may not even be able to bring pen to paper because everything he thinks of seems too inadequate or imprecise. No matter, he can only perceive of himself and reality as grandiose or as worthless and empty. For this reason, every way out of his unbearable self-experience is narcissistic. We call it "negative narcissism" when someone completely devalues himself, experiencing himself as a loser or a sinner or unlucky, capable of perceiving his surrounding environment only in a distorted form. The self-idealizing narcissist tends to be more familiar to us.

Flight into a distorted perception of self fundamentally changes the relationship to other people and to reality outside of one's ego. Focusing all attention and energy on self-idealization is only possible at the expense of interest in other people and other things. We can distinguish *two forms of devaluation* of everything that does not belong to the grandiose ego (see *The Heart of Man*, 1964a, pp. 77–80; *Social Character in a Mexican Village*, 1970b, pp. 254–255; *Modern Man's Pathology of Normalcy*, 1991e [1953], pp. 86–93).

1. In the first form, the narcissistic character does exhibit an—also idealizing—interest in another person or even in many other people, or in a theme or a project, but the interest, the appreciation, and the engagement return to the narcissist like a boomerang. In reality, such people attempt to instrumentalize other people and things for their own

self-aggrandizement, so that the interest in them is really a *self-centered interest*. Many partnerships, parent–child relationships, and professional relationships suffer intensely from such an instrumentalizing, low-grade narcissism, what Fromm also termed *benign narcissism*. Those who are instrumentalized in this way suffer because, despite the proclaimed idealization, they always have the feeling that it is not really about them, but rather about greatness, power, the success of the other. Their only function is to mirror the other in his greatness or to expand and complement it.

From a psychodynamic perspective, the low-grade narcissistic character continuously stabilizes his endangered self by lending aspects of it an inflated meaning and instrumentalizing others to strengthen his sense of himself.

These psychodynamics determine the dominant *character traits of the low-grade narcissistic character*:

- *Overestimation of self*: bragging, emphatic self-confidence, arrogance, self-praise, self-centeredness, self-satisfaction, smugness, self-admiration; incessant subjectivism. The overestimation of self also exists in a negative sense as compulsive rumination, a wallowing in self-recrimination, in the form of moral misgivings; as a preoccupation with mistakes, physical imperfections, illnesses, and disadvantages.
- *A formidable self-centeredness and fixation on the self* (on one's appearance, speech, feelings, ideas, merits); in our era of electronic media, narcissistic self-centeredness tends to express itself in the use of tools with names like iPhone, iTunes, I-Clip, etc.
- *An idealization of others*, to the degree that they mirror and complement oneself; an appreciation of what is familiar and a disdain for the foreign.
- *Disdain and disparagement* for everything beyond the self and of everything that does not mirror the self.
- *Escape into daydreams and imaginary worlds* that allow for heroic fantasies and grandiose role play.

- *Lack of interest and indifference* to everything that is unrelated to oneself or one's own issues.
- *Lack of empathy* and a general incapacity to feel mercy, compassion, or sympathy, to be helpful, or to show social commitment.
- *Ambitious striving for greatness* and perfection, special status, superiority, singularity, excellence (one must be the best, greatest, strongest, most understanding, etc.).
- *Intensely vulnerable to and easily offended* by criticism and failure; incapable of self-critique.
- Special *propensity for depression* when one loses an idealized aspect of the self—for example, one's figure—or when the idealization of another person is no longer possible, because this person goes his own way and extracts himself from instrumentalization (depression not because of an object loss, but a loss of self).
- Extensive *incapacity to sense negatively experienced feelings* (guilt, anxiety, failure, dependency, helplessness, or powerlessness) and to acknowledge them.
- *Striving for self-sufficiency* to avoid dependence on others (not asking, requesting, thanking, apologizing, regretting, reconciling, or repairing).

2. If the first form of devaluation expresses itself as a feigned interest, which is really a lack of interest in everything that is different and refuses to be instrumentalized for one's own grandiosity, the second form of devaluation expresses itself directly and without apology: to secure one's own grandiosity, everything that does not serve this purpose is experienced as a threat, declared an enemy, and held at a distance. It comes to a parting of the ways. At all relationship levels it becomes a matter of either/or: either the other gives himself over so totally to the narcissist that he thinks, feels, acts, and wants exactly the same things, or he will be declared an enemy and belong to the "axis of evil."

If the other, or anything different, can still exist in the presence of the narcissist, then only as an appropriated other in which there is nothing left of his difference (in narcissistic partnerships, this is often experienced as the "great love"). Such a possessive narcissism can be observed not only in partnerships, but in professional relations of dependence, sectarian and fundamentalist movements, as well in parent–child relationships in which the child is only seen as an aspect of one's own grandiosity. A criticism of the child (perhaps by the teacher) is experienced as an attack on the parents (and leads accordingly to parent–teacher conflicts).

But this markedly possessive narcissism, also deemed "malignant" by Fromm, differs greatly from instrumentalizing narcissism not only in interactions with what is outside the self and the other. In marked narcissism, the interaction with oneself also exhibits a heightened grandiosity and a strengthened defense of same which tolerates no questioning. This leads not only to a broad incapacity to be self-critical or endure the criticism of others (strongly marked narcissists are highly resistant to therapy and counseling), but rather because of their exaggerated self-idealization they need to keep every negative experience and self-perception at a distance. As a consequence, all deficits, imperfections, failures, errors, and any weakness in oneself must be denied and projected onto others. The *projection of one's own deficits onto stereotypes of the enemy* and the existential necessity of such stereotypes belong to the marked narcissistic character.

Narcissistic notions of grandeur *conflict* not only with one's own internal differences and with what differentiates others from oneself, but also *with external reality* and facts. These, too, are experienced as threatening and when possible are disavowed. Opportunities today to use social media, and through them *to invent reality anew*, have led to what is called our "post-truth" era. The truth content of information no longer defines itself by objectifiable facts, but rather by the emotional content of the message and the agreement with which it meets in social media. It is no surprise that very intense narcissists, and not only Donald Trump, systematically use this possibility to reconstruct reality in order to eliminate any objective circumstances and facts that oppose their fantasies of grandeur. Constructions that deny one reality only to create new ones have become a tried and true means of populist technique in business, advertising, politics, society, and culture. From a psychological perspective, this new construction of reality, defined by a fantasy of grandeur, always comes at the expense of any true sense of reality, with a loss of reality as its consequence.

A further feature of a strongly marked narcissistic character is a relative *freedom from fear* and simultaneously a permanent *readiness for aggression*. Instead of responding with fear, the narcissist flexes his muscles and becomes aggressive. What is projected is experienced as an external threat to the self. Because this is not a real threat, to which one would usually respond with fear and self-assertion, but rather one's own disavowed, negative shadow side, the threatened self does not respond with fear, but with distancing feelings and affects: disparagement, aggression, demonization, stigmatization, rage, hate, hostility, disgust, etc.

One other feature unfailingly describes a strongly marked narcissism: if the defense of the heightened grandiosity fails and one's *narcissism is violated*, the response is one of *annihilating rage*. There are few situations in which so much destructiveness is as explosively released as with wounded narcissism. Usually, the unbridled rage is directed at those who have violated the narcissism; if this is not possible, then the rage can also be directed at the narcissist himself.

Especially when nonviolence and pacifism form an essential part of one's own grandiose sense of self, wounded narcissism can lead to an "annihilating" fury and to self-destructive depressions that can end in self-harm and suicide. Frequently, such suicidal people kill themselves in a manner that symbolizes a fall from their narcissistic heights into the abyss: they plunge from a highway bridge, tower, or skyscraper into the depths; or they race at high speed into a bridge pillar or, without stopping, into a truck.

The *strongly marked narcissistic* character can be recognized primarily through the following traits:

• In the awareness and *demonstration of greatness*, infallibility, superiority, invulnerability, excellence, and singularity, a sense of being chosen and called, as well as the *avoidance of rivalry* and competition.

- In the *creation, cultivation, and intransigent adherence to stereotypes of enemies* who are made to bear those personal qualities that one must disavow because they contradict one's grandiose sense of self.

- In the *disavowal of one's own feelings of weakness,* finitude, fear, guilt, and failure.

- In strong *distancing feelings such as disgust* toward everything that is incompatible with one's own sense of greatness and for that reason must be "excreted" and projected.

- In a generally unconscious but *fierce envy* toward everyone who has an edge in terms of greatness, vitality, achievement, etc.; since envy would "betray" one's own dissatisfaction and neediness, it must be repressed; often it is only evident in a reaction formation in which envy cannot be felt at all.

- In a *split between good and evil,* in the division of people into those who are on one's side and those who are not ("whoever isn't with me is against me"); in an *either/or attitude,* in a principled and uncompromising nature that denies ambivalence and projects negative aspects of the self.

- In the *aggressive instead of fearful or interested reaction* to everything foreign and outside of the self.

- In the pervasive *tendency to fits of rage* as soon as something does not succeed in a manner that corresponds to one's notions of grandeur.

- In the *avoidance of feelings of dependency* and reliance on others, which is why in interactions with others there is a lack of anything related to questions, requests, thanks, apologies, excuses, regrets, reconciliations, and reparations.

- In the *tendency to make oneself invulnerable and unrivaled* through unequaled perfection and high performance, or by sealing and armoring oneself off, and building a wall around oneself.

- In the *pursuit of narcissistic possession* and narcissistic collusions with other individuals or with collective entities.

- In the *pursuit of total authority* over others and in a lack of shame and ability to respect boundaries.
- In an *extreme irritability* that usually leads to completely disproportionate reactions through which the narcissist terrorizes his surroundings.
- In a *heightened touchiness and oversensitivity* that express an incapacity to handle criticism, and through which the narcissist signals to his environment that any doubt and any critique of his grandiosity should be silenced.
- With strongly marked narcissism, any violation of grandiosity leads to reduced affect regulation, which manifests in *barely controllable rage, fury, and destructiveness toward others and toward oneself.*
- Heightened sensitivity increases the *tendency to avoid confronting reality* and either to exist only in *fantasy* or—especially in our post-factual age—to *reinvent reality according to one's own needs,* which from a psychological and psychiatric perspective leads to a *loss of reality.*

Both forms of the narcissistic character, the low-grade instrument-alizing and the strongly marked possessive narcissism, are non-productive because they hinder man's capacity for growth in his need to satisfy his individual and social sense of identity. The same is true for *group narcissism,* which Fromm described for the first time in 1964 (see *The Heart of Man,* 1964a, pp. 78–87). With the concept of group narcissism, Fromm illustrates the importance that narcissistic leaders and idealized social groups (nations, clubs, associations, parties, etc.) and family ties (clans, extended families, nuclear families) assume in order to compensate for deficits in one's sense of identity.

His argument is that one's own sense of worthlessness is not eliminated by one's *own* ideas of grandiosity, but rather by identifying with the idealization of that group to which one feels a sense of belonging and through which one feels a social sense of identity. According to Fromm, every person is always already a social being, and is related not only to singular individuals but rather to a social group (similar to what sociobiologists posit today with their attachment theory), which is why people do not want to experience their identity solely as individuals, but also—through their group affiliation—as social beings.

With regard to narcissistic group affiliation, Fromm writes:

> Even if one is the most miserable, the poorest, the least respected member of a group, there is compensation for one's miserable condition in feeling "I am a part of the most wonderful group in the world. I, who in reality am a worm, become a giant through belonging to the group." Consequently, the degree of group narcissism is commensurate with the lack real satisfaction in life.
>
> *The Anatomy of Human Destructiveness*, 1973a, p. 230

Deficits in an individual's sense of identity can also be compensated for by identifying with an idealized group leader or group. In fact, this form of narcissism is usually most common in the political arena: from the *Führer* cult and racial delusions of the "Thousand (!) Year Reich" to the right-wing populist movements of the present and the fact that in 2016 almost half the American electorate voted to "Make America great again" and "America first!"

Group narcissism shows character traits and a dynamic similar to what can be observed in narcissistic partner relationships:

- The leader or group must affirm their own superiority and grandiosity and may not show any kind of shortcomings.
- Those who identify with the leader or the group struggle to maintain their grandiosity, train in apologetics, and suppress any questions.
- Any criticism must be kept at a distance from the idealized leader or group, which is why critics are to be muzzled.
- All deficits and mistakes are denied by the leader and the group, and projected onto stereotypes of an enemy.
- Other leaders or groups (nations, milieus, religions, refugees, etc.) are declared enemies from which one must protect oneself and which, when possible, are to be eradicated.

- Group narcissism pretends to be the people's voice, but is in reality anti-democratic.
- It shows no real (social, cultural, political, religious) tolerance and acceptance toward that which is external and foreign.
- Instead of community, group narcissism promotes conflict.
- Nationalism, patriotism, imperialism, racism as well as claims of superiority and infallibility are to be understood and unmasked as variants of collective narcissism.

The *genesis of narcissistic character formations* can be related to very personal circumstances, which is why Fromm speaks of an individual narcissistic character formation. When a parent mirrors to a child or a spouse, or a superior mirrors to an adult, that they are only a burden and of no use, often the only refuge through which to secure a scrap of self-worth is grandiose fantasies—with all of the consequences that such a character formation then has for interactions with oneself and other people.

What interested Fromm much more, however, is the question of how a narcissistic social character is formed. If many, or even sometimes the majority, in a society or social group possess a narcissistic character, then this must relate to a mass experience of diminishment and a negative sense of identity as outgrowths of serious economic and social changes. Only this can explain the occurrence of a mass narcissistic character formation.

The narcissistic social character orientation indicates a psychic structural formation that attempts to remedy a deficient sense of identity. For that reason, the origins of a narcissistic character orientation are also to be found in those social character formations that arise at the expense of a growth-oriented sense of identity and self-worth.

Consequences already became clear in the psychodynamics of the marketing orientation. In the marketing of one's own personality, an orientation around success in the marketplace is usually only possible at the expense of an authentic sense of identity, because success is dependent upon the adoption of marketable personality traits. As long as personality training can leverage one's unschooled, stunted competencies and soft skills toward growth, such adoption has a growth-promoting effect on one's sense of identity and will not contribute toward self-alienation.

But, if anything, this is the exception. Generally, it is a matter of "competencies" that have nothing to do with one's personality. The marketing of one's personality means turning oneself into a product for purchase, and for that reason one trains those personal traits with which one can succeed in a particular market—independent of one's own personal characteristics, capacities, and problems. Anything that could interfere with economic aspirations of success is to be put aside, repressed, and denied. In reality, as we have seen, the marketing orientation corrupts any sense of identity and impedes the ability of the psychic capacity for growth to experience its own powers as a part of one's coherent self.

The successful marketing character experiences himself consciously as someone who is capable of slipping into every desired personality possible, and attributes his success and worth to this ability. He is usually also conscious of the fact that his sense of self-worth depends upon the response of the market, and he therefore must remain up-to-date at all costs and permanently optimize himself in order to stay fit for the market and his profession.

The manner in which the marketing-oriented person goes on vacation supports this analysis. Vacation is usually not for "relaxation"; it is also not a performance-free zone in which one can finally return to oneself; more often, a vacation is designed to be just as performance- and success-oriented, if by other means, so that one can congratulate oneself about everything that one experienced and "achieved."

Only a few marketing-oriented people are truly aware of the fact that their positive sense of identity and self-worth is in growing measure completely dependent on a response of success and barely has anything to do any longer with one's own interests, feelings, desires, and capacities. That is why there is hardly any sense of meaning in their lives and work; there is a lack of "resonant experiences" based on an inner emotional relatedness, as impressively described by Hartmut Rosa (2016), which would allow them to overcome their alienation. Instead, the marketing-oriented person sees his own needs, feelings, aspirations, and longings as something external.

As long as this response can be produced, a deficient sense of identity usually remains unconscious, because the echo of success allows one to experience a feeling of self-worth. If success is likely to remain absent, or, for whatever reasons, really never does appear, then the development of narcissistic fantasies of grandeur are often the chosen method to avoid a mental breakdown.

The interesting point here is not so much whether narcissistic compensation develops only after the absence of success or before. There is much to suggest that the marketing character fosters, indeed requires, the development of a narcissistic social character formation, in order not to wind up on the losing side in the case of failure. What is decisive is that the marketing-oriented person does not experience himself and his self-worth based on the exercise of his own powers, but rather obtains these experiences externally and thereby suffers from a deficient self.

It is also important to consider that marketing strategies increasingly serve a narcissistic logic. Grandiosity, premium quality, super organic, excellence, the best of the best, the most ecologically friendly with the guaranteed best price, etc., are promoted and sold. Success begins when narcissistic needs and demands have been met.

Undoubtedly, major economic and social changes in the capitalist market economy play a crucial role in explaining the widespread formation of the narcissistic social character. This also is true in individual cases where a mixture of social and individual experiences of devaluation may lead to a narcissistic character formation. Major socio-economic changes were already briefly addressed in the description of the marketing orientation.

From a socio-psychoanalytic perspective, a new social character orientation has since developed. Its fundamental goal is no longer success, but rather the wish to do everything new and differently, with autonomy: we should have the independence to construct our limited surrounding reality, but also our own limited personality, anew and differently. I call this the "ego orientation." This new social character formation described in the following section is unthinkable without what we describe as the "digital revolution." Indeed, it is these technical innovations that have led and are still leading to serious changes in all areas of life. Their psychological relevance should be briefly mentioned here (for more detail, see Funk, 2011, pp. 43–82).

Digital technology, electronic media, and networking technology have made possible new products and production methods that show us at every turn how manmade digital, electronic, and media marvels have the capacity to do so much more than man ever could with his own physical, emotional, and intellectual powers. This devaluation of man's unique powers means that they become ever more "deactivated" with one's own "externalized" capacity now sought in technological marvels.

In the ego-oriented character, there is a sort of symbiosis with and existential dependence on technological capability. The term "iPhone" captures this well: who am I if I cannot have an I-Phone? The I, or ego, and the medium have entered into a symbiosis. As long as we have this technological capability at our disposal, an impending incapacity— namely, the inability to draw on our own cognitive and emotional strengths any longer—does not surface. In the marketing orientation, "success" is the cure that prevents any awareness of our loss of self; in the ego orientation, the medium is the cure that protects us from feeling unmotivated, empty, and isolated.

Of course, there are many more reasons why people today have conscious and unconscious deficits in their sense of identity. Every narcissistic character formation—also that of group narcissism— represents a psychically nonproductive processing of experiences of devaluation. The contemporary problem lies above all in the actual devaluation of one's own capacities of growth in the face of a suggestive promotion of the superiority of technological solutions and in their actual superiority in certain areas, which is barely absorbed on a conscious level. The increase in narcissistic character formations shows that man unconsciously feels himself a failure and, without success and technological capabilities at his disposal, helpless and powerless.

Every narcissistic character formation represents a mode that hinders man's growth capacity and thus his ability to satisfy his need for an individual and social sense of identity. The most diverse forms of narcissism are—simply put—nonproductive because they strongly reduce the interest in and for the other that all living beings share, and, sometimes with strongly marked narcissism, turn it into its opposite.

Narcissistic character formations always come at the expense of any genuine interest in other people and for everything that goes beyond the comfortably familiar. They represent, even in their weak form, a major obstacle to the capacity to grow psychologically. Man can only grow psychologically when he is capable of breaking new ground, and when he wants to become familiar with what is foreign—in others and in himself. Because people differ from each other in multiple ways, an interest in the other is absolutely necessary for social coexistence.

In every form of narcissism, the other's difference loses its attractiveness and society's atomization advances. The stronger the narcissism, the more the lack of interest in the other turns into a hostility toward everything that is not one's own. Society's loss of solidarity evolves into battles between narcissistic groups within a nation, and into more or less hostile demarcations between other nations, ethnicities, and cultures. The grave social and political consequences of narcissistic character formations show that "narcissism is the opposite pole to objectivity, reason and love" (*The Sane Society*, 1955a, p. 36).

In light of *the art of living*, it is important to note that narcissistic character formations result from deficits in one's sense of identity and self-worth, and that a deficient sense of identity is connected with the experience (sometime self-inflicted) of devaluation. Some concluding remarks that I offer with regard to the narcissistic character orientation, and possibilities for reactivating a sense of identity and self-worth, are intentionally restricted to the question of interacting with narcissistic people.

In the art of living, such individual efforts are often only effective when the devaluing conditions that lead to a conscious and unconscious negative sense of self and self-worth are also changed. I discuss this, at least to some degree, in relation to a weakened sense of identity in the marketing and ego orientations.

When engaging with one's own narcissism, and especially the narcissism of other people (partners, children, clients, etc.), one should always keep in mind that any criticism and irritation only strengthens the (often unconscious) distress of being unable to have a positive sense of identity and hence contributes to an intensification of narcissism. For that reason, the following two approaches are often as a rule *counterproductive*:

- Any attempt to force change (even with very well-intentioned advice) leads to aggressive or even enraged reactions, to an intensification of grandiose fantasies and/or to an even stronger blockade.
- Although often used as a method of change, the suggestive strengthening of self-esteem flatters the narcissist, but also generally leads to a mirroring of the grandiose self and thus to a welcome reinforcement of narcissism by a co-narcissist. The problem that the narcissist cannot tolerate any deficiency is not addressed.

Productive strategies of change aim to integrate deficient aspects of the personality into conscious experience and self-esteem. Only this can reduce the necessity for flight into grandiose notions of the self as well as the necessity of projecting disavowed aspects onto the environment.

- This requires that one does not defend oneself against narcissistic hostility, devaluation, rage, and the production of stereotypes, but rather that one remain open to them with understanding. One must be able to feel: this aggressive, dismissive, arrogant, provocative person in reality feels injured, disappointed, and hurt.
- It does not matter if this is justified or unjustified.

- In such nonjudgmental empathy lies the key to establishing a relationship with the disavowed negative sense of identity and the deficient parts of the personality. What Fromm meant by "stop judging" (*Dealing with the Unconscious in Psychotherapeutic Practice*, 1992g [1959], p. 106) was illustrated in the Introduction under the heading Letting Someone Sense: "This is you".

- Psychotherapeutic experience indicates the actual difficulty is that empathic access to the split-off side is first rejected (perhaps by demeaning comments about the therapist, by aggressive reactions, or even by not coming to therapy); here patience and stamina are required. Sometimes resistance to letting someone else feel one's low self-worth can only be given up when the narcissist can sense that the other knows this sort of distress (perhaps because something humiliating happened to him, too).

- In parallel to the efforts to liberate the narcissist from his "splendid isolation" through a nonjudgmental empathy, so that his interest in other people and things external to him becomes palpable again, it is necessary to make past and present concrete experiences of devaluation (for example, in professional, familial, and religious contexts) conscious; there are also opportunities and chances to help the person achieve a realistic (and this usually means more modest) sense of self-esteem.

- What applies to working with the narcissistic grandiosity of the individual, is in principle also valid for *interacting with the narcissism of groups*. A pitched battle against nationalistic and racist narcissists is as a rule counterproductive and advisable only when social cooperation has been severely impaired; otherwise, here, too, a nonjudgmental empathy with these groups' experience of devaluation and the elimination of the economic and social dynamic of devaluation are key in depriving group narcissism of its oxygen.

Fromm identified and described still other nonproductive social character orientations, if in less detail than the three introduced here.

Among them are the *hoarding character orientation*, in which people do not exercise their capacities, but rather want to collect and possess, following the model of an economy that lives from the accumulation of capital and requires for its success frugal people who expend nothing, including their own talents (see *Man for Himself*, 1947a, pp. 65–67).

Lastly, at the start of the 1960s, Fromm discovered necrophilia and the *necrophilous social character orientation* (*The Heart of Man*, 1964a, pp. 37–45) and described them in depth in his book *The Anatomy of Human Destructiveness* (1973a). Necrophilia is "the passion to transform that which is alive into something unalive" (1973a, p. 369; see Funk, 2002). The triumphant advance of machines, technology, and techniques, the reification of entire life processes, and the desire and ability to predict everything, determine not only the economy and society, science, and culture, but are reflected in a social character orientation that is drawn more to the lifeless than to the living. For that reason, it attempts to impede systematically all intrinsic powers that express an unpredictable aliveness. That feelings and affective impulses are primarily at stake is shown by the way in which the nonproductive quality of the necrophilic social character orientation comes at the expense of man's own emotional powers.

Economic and social developments since the death of Fromm in 1980 have led to the emergence of an additional social character orientation, what I call the "ego orientation." I explore this in depth in my book *Ich und Wir. Psychoanalyse des postmodernen Menschen* [*I and We. Psychoanalysis of the Postmodern Man*] (Funk, 2005). In my book *Der entgrenzte Mensch* [*Man Without Boundaries*] (Funk, 2011) I analyze the consequences of the ego orientation for the new mental construction of man (see the English summary in Funk, 2014). Following an empirical study of the SIGMA Institute in Mannheim (see the summary by Frankenberger, 2007), as of 2006 almost 20 percent of adults in Germany exhibited dominant features of this ego orientation. The orientation is especially prominent in those occupations, age groups, and social milieus that on the one hand deal with digital technology and electronic media, and on the other with the staging of reality in the creative sector, in the entertainment industry, and in the media.

Since this orientation is gaining importance and since I developed it with the help of Frommian concepts, I offer it here as a further illustration of how a social character orientation may contribute to a society's well-being but hinder man's own ability to thrive.

The ego orientation—at the expense of ego strength

Many researchers have identified and described how people have come to a new internalized way of relating to reality, to other people, and to themselves, and this is reflected in concepts such as "risk society" (Beck, 1992), "experience-driven society" (Schulze, 1992), "corrosion of character" (Sennett, 1998), or "liquid modernity" (Bauman, 2000). Psychologically speaking, the changes have been described primarily as new personality types, or, following Fromm, as new social character orientations. They range from Robert Lifton's "protean self" (1993) to Martin Dornes's "postheroic personality" (2012); in the tradition of Fromm, Michael Maccoby discusses the "interactive character" (1999), while I myself presented for the first time in 2005 the "ego-oriented character" in its conscious and unconscious facets (Funk, 2005; 2014).

Ego-oriented people are overly sensitive to anything that could limit or bind them, or when others expect a limit or a commitment. They aspire to a limitless freedom that—unlike egoists or narcissists—they grant every other person as well.

To live autonomously, ego-oriented people consistently avoid *limitations* and *predetermined boundedness* to something or someone: they are oriented around their own ego. What motivates their thought, feeling, and action most deeply is self-determination: *I* want to determine what reality is, who I am, with whom I interact, and the people who suit me. An individual sense of identity should not be restricted by natural handicaps or social restraints. This represents a new quality of freedom. Should obligations, limitations, and commitments arise, they need to be made flexible, one needs to *un*bind and remove limits on the self, either by concretely eliminating these factors or by replacing them with performative and virtual reconstructions of reality. (Removing limits does not mean transcending and overcoming them, but rather the elimination of what limits or binds one.)

Along with a striving for limitlessness, the *desire to invent a new and different reality* is the second discernible trait of the ego-oriented character. Everything must be reinvented, reorganized, restructured, solved creatively with the help of today's technological, above all digital and electronic, possibilities in the shape of performative and virtual constructions of reality and with the help of appropriate programs, communications technologies, methods, manuals, didactics, trainings, etc.

This is how new firms are set up. "Images" must be developed and employees presented with not only a "corporate identity" but a "corporate culture." Politics, education, family—everything must be reinvented. These "technological solutions" are extremely beneficial in many areas, and everyday life, especially business, media, science, and research, is unimaginable without them.

As I see it, the ego orientation, especially noteworthy in its striving for limitlessness and technical creativity, exists in two versions, one active and one passive. Similar to the authoritarian character, who either exerts a sadistic dominance or is masochistically submissive, the *active* ego-oriented person wants to reinvent himself and his environment, his lifestyle and his entertainment, and thereby produce unlimited realities, feelings, and experiences; the *passive* ego-oriented person, in contrast, wants to partake *autonomously* in these newly constructed realities, choosing which living environment, lifestyle, brand, and style of music *suits* him.

The desired sense of identity is also correspondingly different. The passive ego-oriented person inhabits the position of I by feeling connected and belonging. Only in this manner can he live out his boundlessness and freedom. In experiencing a feeling of "we," he perceives his ego. By feeling connected he feels free. As mutually exclusive as the ego orientation and boundedness are, because boundedness signifies dependence and therefore limitation, the experience of connectivity is of central importance in overcoming one's own limitations.

In addition, people with a strong ego orientation who try to live without regard for the demands and conditions of others are always in danger of socially isolating themselves. A society of ego-oriented individuals is threatened by a very different sort of atomization than were the premodern collectives threatened by the loss of inclusion. The imperative of "connectedness" (Hüther and Spannbauer, 2012) is today an essential aspect of the ego orientation, in which *autonomous* connectedness is at stake. This explains, too, why engagement in associations has become so difficult and hardly anyone wants to be forced into following obligatory association rules.

There exists therefore not only a new "ego experience," but also a new "we experience," a new sort of sociality and sense of community that emerges in a new "feeling of we" that refuses being tied down but wants—autonomous—connection.

Some particularly typical *character traits* include:

- A *pleasure in doing*, managing, performing, being creative, producing, and applying expertise (in the active version) and an *attraction to that which has been produced*, experienced, performed, to that which is enlivening and stimulating (with the passive ego-oriented person).
- A *fascination with feelings*: unlike with the marketing orientation, feelings play a very important role for ego-oriented people. They show an (active) emotional strength, live from their gut, or perform feelings by emotionalizing entertainment and communication (for example, with help from emojis); passive ego-oriented people in contrast are moved by manufactured feelings in order to partake in them and be able to empathize. The great market opportunity of contemporary cultural production lies in the presentation and selling of feelings in the staged worlds of crime shows, soap operas, and musicals, in heart-wrenching

love stories, in gossip columns about celebrities, or in an emotionalized news report.

- *Sociability* replaces in large part what until now had been understood as relationships and attention to them, enabling a *noncommittal connection*: precisely because it is not about traditional emotional ties but rather the cultivation of contacts, people seek autonomous connections, but avoid anything having to do with the desire for a relationship: obligations, expectations of dependability, or even a sustained wish for intimacy.

- This different art of relating means that ego-oriented people *never hold a grudge* and, despite the collapse of a partnership, remain friends with their exes. *Jealousy* is usually not an issue. *Sexually*, it is important to feel free and to actualize oneself. Everything is permitted, including abstinence.

- The *striving for limitlessness* and the experience of no boundaries: ego-oriented people love what is risky, edgy, out of bounds, offensive, unconventional, impossible—whether in sport, literature, film, or on vacation. Time and space also know no limits, so that each person gets to decide when day is and when night.

- *Tolerance of and a respect for the other as well as cooperativeness and fairness* are noticeable character traits of ego-oriented people, as are *apathy* and *indifference* toward anything that doesn't suit them.

- Ego-oriented people display a different *sense of community* and *sociability*: social or political engagement is not defined by a feeling of responsibility or duty, but rather by the value of the engagement experience and the possibility to be thereby connected and actualize oneself.

- A *yearning for the positive*: ego-oriented people practice positive thinking, positive feeling, and positive action, avoid any sort of conflict, and do not know a negative sense of self.

The ego orientation is also the result of a *social imprint* in which an internal character orientation develops in response to what a society requires of human effort for its own success. Below, I discuss two of the many reasons that facilitate this new character orientation. (See Funk, 2011, pp. 43–61.)

Successful business endeavors have long recognized that the production of goods and services does not promise success, but rather *the production of reality* in the form of experiences, emotions, living environments, and lifestyles. The production of experiences and lifestyles should give certain target groups the opportunity to feel at home in these realities and to identify with them. The endpoint of such a development is a world in which practically every activity becomes a *staged* and *appropriated* experience. Life itself becomes a commodity. The communications and culture industries produce it for us, and we buy life, experiences, and feelings from them by paying for access to the experiences they promote.

The economy generates and stages realities without the consumer ever feeling the need to measure these preprocessed experiences against a pre-existing reality. The appeal of creating a new and different reality, which typifies this character orientation, is predominantly the result of an identification process with an economic necessity.

Equally important for the rise of the ego orientation are the overwhelming achievements over the last decades in the areas of *digital technology, networking technology*, and *electronic media*. They are an essential precondition for the current elimination of boundaries of space and time, for split-second knowledge and information transfers, for imaging procedures that open up completely new perspectives (for example in brain research), for measurement techniques never dreamed possible (which for example open the gateway to nanotechnology), for communication, and knowledge acquisition or entertainment independent of space and time. Without electronic media as well as digital and network technologies, the mobilization, globalization, and flexibilization of almost all production processes, and the people involved with them, would not be possible; there would be no genetic decoding and no space exploration.

The digital revolution and its fantastical computing, staging, and simulation technologies opened up unimagined possibilities for creating a new and different reality. Using them is highly attractive, not only for ego-oriented people. With the help of manmade products, people today are able to shape their own and the surrounding reality in new, better, more impressive, competent, invigorating, colorful, emotional, and entertaining ways than if they were to rely on their own—admittedly, relatively modest—human powers. Since the invention of the first tools, man has created and shaped reality with his human capacities, that is, with his own sensory and bodily, emotional, and intellectual powers as well as with what he has produced, that is with his "manufactured capacities." In the past, his "manufactured capacities" (in the form of tools, machines, and techniques) gained importance, but they never put into serious question the exercise of man's own powers.

Psychologically, the digital revolution has meant a radical shift. With the employment of "manufactured capacities" in the shape of technology and techniques, management tools, manuals, and programs, man is not only *capable of much more*, but "manufactured capacities" are now active in those areas that until now had been exclusively, or almost exclusively, guided by the practice of "human" capacities: in the *realm of one's own personality and in the realm of personal and social communities*. Digital technology, networking technology, and electronic media have made entirely new *psychological and social technologies* possible.

With personality training and corresponding management programs, self-perception and decision-making are optimized, social competencies developed, cognitive and communicative abilities improved. The facility to learn and tolerate conflict increases, and leadership qualities are acquired. Psychological techniques in the realm of personal skills offer what social techniques offer in the realm of human coexistence and the organization of the social. Almost everything today is described by or linked with concepts of "steering," "program," or "management."

The psychologically problematic aspect of the reconstruction of reality relates above all to the *mental reconstruction of one's own personality*. Here, too, the starting point is that one's own personality feels too limited and ambiguous, even counterproductive. A solution is sought that attempts to eliminate personality's imprint by appropriate neural and psychological structure formations.

The following five aspects of personality illustrate man's mental reconstruction:

1. The capacity to live based on *one's own motivating forces*.
2. The capacity to experience oneself as *identical to others*.
3. The capacity to be in *relationships*.
4. The capacity to *self-regulate normatively*.
5. The capacity to *feel authentically*.

1. Let us begin with our *own motivating forces*: all that allows us to act on our own initiative, that motivates, enlivens, and interests us, can barely keep up with those thrilling, inspiring, and stimulating effects of the staged and virtual entertainments on offer. Our own motivating powers are exercised less and less, becoming "deactivated." We can recognize this deactivation in the fact that we first need something interesting in order to feel any real interest. Acknowledging desire and doing something about it frequently require some sort of "inspiration," something that literally breathes life into one—this is even the case in the need for intimacy or sexual satisfaction. The trajectory of activation is the exact opposite of the deactivation of one's own motivating forces: stimulation, activity, effectiveness, creative power—instead of emanating from the person, they emanate from the entertainment on offer.

2. With regard to a *sense of identity*: someone who wants to experience himself as truly free must leave behind his familiar *sense of identity*, that is relinquish a defined self. Depending on the occasion, situation, and inclination, a newly invented self and a newly "manufactured" personality replace the original self. When ego-oriented people speak of "self-actualization," they mean something different from the actualization of their own unique self. The boundaries of the self are eliminated in a new creation no longer tied to its history. Yet the demand remains that whatever the process of reinvention, they be themselves. The same is true for ego-oriented people's understanding of authenticity. Someone who cannot be other than he is is not authentic. Instead,

authentic is someone who is capable of consistently and skillfully performing or simulating a self without recognizing that there is a "singularity" in himself and others.

3. With regard to the capacity to *be in relationships*, we see in the reinvention of personality a striving to eliminate boundaries primarily in the way that those indispensable forces of emotional attachment— feelings of longing, missing, remembering, trusting, intimacy and harmony, grief, empathic caring, shared sorrow, etc.—are seen as too limiting and are experienced as fostering dependency. The limitations of one's own powers of attachment show in the way that the latter are fused with jealous, demeaning, or hostile feelings, or feelings of inferiority, which disrupt relationships.

Ego-oriented people thus strive to "de-tach" from their emotional powers of attachment, in order to stay "connected without attachment" in a completely self-determined form of relatedness. While they do develop relationships, it is not with their emotional powers of attachment, but rather through the cultivation of contacts. Unattached connections through social media have the great advantage that they are easy to control. At any given moment, one can put contacts at a distance and determine when, how much, and for how long a relationship is desired.

Cultivating social-media contacts is a new form of everyday relationships and is also experienced this way. The more followers and friends one has, the longer one spends in chat rooms or on Facebook, the more photos seen through WhatsApp, and the longer the list of email and text recipients, the more related and connected one feels.

4. With regard to the *capacity normatively to regulate ourselves as well as each other*, the question arises as to the fate of the psychic structures of the superego, ego ideal, and conscience as the boundaries around these parts of the personality are eliminated. As part of our psychic endowment, they represent a handicap and a basis from which one must detach if one wants to live an autonomous life without feelings of permanent or recurring anxiety, guilt, and shame. What takes the place of this inner system of regulation? Even people who cannot tolerate limits do not dispute that life and living together must somehow be

regulated and that we must orient ourselves around something. Indeed, they want nothing more than *autonomous* orientation and regulation.

The call today is made for regulations, new orientations, and values, for medical and scientific ethics, for occupational and professional standards, for political and corporate correctness, for consensus, mission statements, and role models. The need for consultants, advisors, coaches, and ethics has to do with unbounded man's detachment from internalized values and orientations.

5. Finally, *one's own feelings* are also in play with the mental reconstruction of personality. Along with desires and fantasies, feelings belong to the most important means of psychic expression. That is why sensing, sharing, and articulating feelings, instead of repressing them, are essential. As clinical experiences with neurotic and psychosomatic states of suffering show, this is also true when the expression of certain feelings is socially taboo.

With regard to their own feelings, ego-oriented people find themselves in a dilemma: on the one hand, precisely their own feelings make them aware of their limitations and attachments, and thus they want to be rid of them. On the other, feelings are something highly individual, alive and enlivening. They offer an extremely effective way autonomously to create reality, contact, and communication, and to connect with other people.

The ego-oriented person solves this dilemma by giving way to all things feeling, not by staking a claim to his own feelings, but rather either through *an active* performance or simulation or what may be completely different feelings, or *a passive* connection to the fashionable feelings being promoted—instead of his own pain, he feels someone else's. As already noted, business has ramped up the production of psychic realities—of feelings, passions, and real experiences—and stops at nothing to make the consumer believe that he needs these manufactured psychic realities, experiences, feelings, and passions in order to be satisfied, effective, cooperative, and happy.

Autonomously producing or feeling someone else's staged and simulated feelings, instead of sensing one's own authentic feelings, is attractive for two other reasons: one can escape negative feelings toward others and oneself, and one can deceptively experience socially taboo feelings—such as vengeful or murderous feelings—without needing to acknowledge these feelings as one's own.

It is often not at the individual's discretion if he empathizes with staged or simulated feelings. Especially in light of the demands of successful management, a smooth organization of work flow and a community life free of conflict, more and more people are expected to undergo the appropriate personality training. Living with the help of simulated feelings offers the (albeit questionable) "advantage" of experiencing contentment and happiness independently of authentic feelings.

People today are expected to be always friendly, cooperative, fair, appreciative, performance-oriented, and motivated, not to feel inferior or show aggression toward others. Psychologists, coaches, and personality trainers work unrelentingly on programs that lead people to think and feel only positively, to shower those around them with empathy, praise, and appreciation, to forego aggression and to rise above any self-doubt. Psychologically, this only works when negatively experienced (hurtful, painful) feelings toward others and oneself are largely blocked.

Even if it seems to those with virtual feelings like a message from another world, it can hardly be denied: someone can only value and love himself and others when he doesn't block out the dark sides, the difficulties and criticisms of self and others, but rather accepts them, values them, and perhaps is even capable of loving them. Everything else is—as Barbara Ehrenreich (2010) showed—an idealizing distortion of reality in which positive thinking deteriorates into ideology. This goes along with a massive suppression of anything that contradicts the idealization. Suppressed aspects of reality—as already became clear with the narcissistic character formation—do not simply vanish from the world. They are projected onto scapegoats and enemies, where they are devalued, fought, and kept at a distance. Those who block out what is difficult and unbearable make themselves dependent on stereotypes of an enemy.

The mental reconstruction of personality is no longer a Utopia. Today we are in a position largely to dispense with our own human powers. All we have to do is learn which tools, trainings, guides, manuals, techniques, and tricks to use in which situation. Learning is relegated to know-how, and thanks to search engines, we need not "know-how" to get ahold of know-how any more. The art of living is reduced— according to the ego-oriented vision—to the application of given solutions.

The ego-oriented character differs from the productive character precisely in the way that he *attempts to substitute* his "human" capacities with all-powerful, "manufactured" capacities, while the productive character uses "manufactured" capacities in order to empower his "human" capacities. The productive character, for example, wants to practice expanding his musical gifts with the help of a synthesizer that produces new soundscapes.

The degree to which "manufactured" capacities express an ego orientation or to which someone uses "manufactured" capacities to optimize his "human" ones can be determined by visualizing what a weekend without electricity (and a battery) would look like. Such a visualization can quickly make clear if a lack of electronic media, contacts, internet, entertainment, news, and films leaves one feeling alienated, empty, helpless and "out of one's mind," or if one knows what to do with oneself and others, and can still draw on one's own physical, psychic, and mental powers.

To understand the *psychic dynamics* that lead to the ego orientation, and to gain insight into how ego-oriented people unconsciously perceive their ego, it helps to take a look at some behavioral issues that suggest a diminished ego.

- Ego-oriented people always attempt to avoid all of life's contradictions. They refuse to accept that their partner, their parents, their children, their work can be satisfying *and* stressful, a blessing *and* a curse. They only acknowledge the positive, while they steer clear of difficulties, criticism, and conflict.

- They have an extremely difficult time recognizing limits and their own limitations, or submitting to fate, accepting restrictions, and being satisfied with less.
- Even harder is the recognition and toleration of negative feelings such as psychic pain, helplessness, passivity, impotence, and isolation.
- The already mentioned difficulty with attachment and an inability to sense feelings of longing, fidelity, intimacy, and affection correlate with a clear impairment in sensing feelings of separation—grief, loneliness, loss, disappointment.
- Another striking feature is usually the counterphobic response to those affects central to the development of the ego, such as anxiety, guilt, and shame. Instead of feeling fear, they seek a thrill; instead of admitting weakness, they show a confidence that brooks no self-doubt; instead of hiding their eyes in shame, their eyes feast on the shameless.
- Obvious, too, is the difficulty experienced by many ego-oriented people in living on the basis of their own internalized norms and ideals. They rely heavily on auxiliary egos and auxiliary superegos in the form of advisors, ethical regulations, value systems, or coaching.

The psychic development of a strong ego depends on many factors and experiences, and manifests itself in a range of capabilities and functions. *Indicators of ego strength* include, for example, the ability:

- to differentiate clearly and accurately between one's own reality and the one that surrounds us, that means without denial or distortion;
- to distinguish the worlds of imagination and fantasy from reality, and to use fantasy without escaping from reality;
- to separate what one wants of others and oneself from how others and oneself actually are;
- to be satisfied with less, accepting limitations and suffering;
- to not only talk about ideals and values but actually to practice them;

- to modulate and control impulses and affects;
- to acknowledge positive as well as negative perceptions of self and others;
- to experience thinking, feeling, and acting as a unity, and to put into action what one holds to be right;
- to withstand criticism, failure, and disappointment;
- to risk, address, and endure conflict;
- to be autonomous and self-reliant as well as accept necessary dependencies;
- to be alone while recognizing the desire for closeness and unity;
- to attach and separate, without giving up or losing oneself.

All of this (and more) indicates a strong ego. Someone with these abilities is a "master" at being human, as none of these capacities can be "manufactured." This concretization of what ego strength means leads to the conclusion that the ego orientation is in reality often a desperate attempt to compensate for an increasingly unconscious ego weakness, which, with the help of "manufactured" capacities, is able to appear self-confident and strong.

Psychologically, the performance of an omnipotent ego needs to balance out a lack of relatedness and attachment to inner psychic structures and motivating forces—with the result that in reality the ego becomes even weaker and more dependent on "manufactured" capacities. The central importance of autonomy for the active and passive forms of ego orientation, which suggest a very spontaneous and self-determined subject, is really a rationalization that must conceal a dependence on "manufactured" capacities and prevents it from becoming conscious.

The ego-oriented person cannot become aware that there has been a general shift in leadership roles: he no longer experiences himself as a subject who is led by his own powers—ideas, aspirations, desires, expressions of will, etc. Instead, he is led by "manufactured" instruments and their inherent capacities. Here we can understand why the ego-oriented person wants to be connected without being attached. Without connection, he has no access to "manufactured" capacities.

In the art of living according to Fromm, an important question remains. How is it possible, under such social and characterological preconditions, to reactivate the *psychic* capacity for growth and thereby *strengthen the productive orientation*?

In all social character orientations, the *general goal* of strengthening the productive orientation is to activate the psychic powers of growth. In the case of the ego orientation, however, we speak of reactivating these powers and overcoming an ego weakness that corresponds to a deactivation of one's own mental and psychic powers.

A general direction for (re-)strengthening the ego can be specified, for example:

- by the willingness to expose oneself to physical, mental, and intellectual effort;
- by the practice of craftsmanship and musical skills;
- by visualizations in which one attempts to put oneself in the position of one's partner, opponent, subordinate, or someone who has failed;
- by sympathy and empathy with people experiencing loss or suffering;
- by detecting one's own illusions and the lies one lives;
- by becoming aware of what separates oneself from familial, social, and cultural standards and values;
- by addressing and working through conflicts;
- by experiments in living one's own convictions;
- by critical attention to one's own daydreams and fantasies, and to the fictional worlds of film and literature that move one deeply;
- by a sensitivity to impressions that arise after attending events or being together with others;
- by accepting negative feelings like irritation, rage, jealousy, grief, hate;
- by admitting to others feelings of fear, guilt, and shame;
- by intentional time alone;
- by "detox" experiments: no entertainment through music, TV, or DVDs; not using a mobile phone; no contacts through social

media; no sending or receiving mails or texts; no alcoholic drinks; no distractions; for once, not wanting to experience anything . . .

The art of living according to Fromm always leads us back to enabling the psychic capacity for growth, that is, the productive orientation of character, to become dominant in the face of individual and social impediments. The discussion about the four orientations should have clarified the obstructive role that nonproductive social character orientations play in this.

It is important to keep in mind that no one is simply a reflection of dominant economic and social interests. Almost all people have internalized a mix of diverse, in part contradictory, interests of specific groups. Their behavior is also not solely decided by social character orientations, but rather is determined by many, often very productive individual character traits.

The uniqueness of Fromm's approach remains in understanding the individual primarily as a social being who is simultaneously determined by passionate forces of which he is often not conscious. Precisely this makes it so difficult to develop a productive orientation. To use Fromm's own words:

> The average person, while he thinks he is awake, actually is half asleep. By "half asleep" I mean that his contact with reality is a very partial one; most of what he believes to be reality (outside or inside of himself) is a set of fictions which his mind constructs. He is aware of reality only to the degree to which his social functioning makes it necessary.
>
> *Psychoanalysis and Zen Buddhism*, 1960a, p. 60

In the opening chapter, we saw how Fromm himself exemplified a "direct encounter." The closing chapter focuses on ways that can lead to a direct encounter, and we again begin with a discussion of Fromm himself.

Figure 6 Fromm meditating, 1968. © Lit Fromm Estate.

5

Ways toward Direct Encounter

Erich Fromm's guides on the way toward direct encounter

In my own encounters with Fromm, it almost never happened that he tried to influence me directly—with one exception: he repeatedly and emphatically recommended that I read one particular book. Although Fromm did not share the political conclusions drawn by Johann Jakob Bachofen in his studies on "mother right," he was so fascinated by his findings about early matriarchal societies that he urged me to read at least the foreword of Bachofen's *Mutterrecht und Urreligion* (Bachofen, 1927, pp. 87–156).

His second reading recommendation was Karl Marx, to whose early writings he returned time and again (and which he himself had published for the first time in English in 1961—see *Marx's Concept of Man*, 1961b). In Fromm's opinion, anyone interested in man's self-realization must read the *Economic and Philosophical Manuscripts* (Marx, 1968). In his words,

> what drew me to him was primarily his philosophy and his vision of socialism, which expressed, in secular form, the idea of human self-realization, of total humanization, the idea of a human being whose goal is vital self-expression and not the acquisition and accumulation of dead, material things.
>
> *In the Name of Life*, 1974b, p. 102

The next recommendation, too, belonged to Fromm's almost daily reading in those years: Meister Eckhart's sermons and treatises. In letters to personal friends, Fromm would report repeatedly that he and his wife were reading Eckhart's sermons together. The book *To Have Or to Be?*, which originated during this time, was first planned as a book about Meister Eckhart and Karl Marx because both spoke of the alternative between "having" or "being." This dichotomy captured well what Fromm had developed over decades in his contrasting orientations of the productive and nonproductive characters, which is why a book about Meister Eckhart and Karl Marx ultimately became a book about the character orientations of having or being.

The fourth book Fromm simply gave me, remarking that the exercises described therein were very helpful to him. He thus recommended to me not only certain readings, but also exercises. As much as reading can bring about a direct encounter with the self, themes, and those who have mastered the art of living, more is needed: namely, practice and guidance from these masters of life.

The book that Fromm gave me was titled *The Heart of Buddhist Meditation* and was written by Nyānaponika Mahāthera (1973). I had already come across this name in the manuscript of *To Have Or to Be?*, which he had given me to read. In the manuscript was a chapter with the heading "Steps to Being" in which Fromm introduced the Buddhist teaching of mindfulness as Nyānaponika described it in *The Heart of Buddhist Meditation* and demonstrated through the example of particular exercises. (Shortly before the printing of *To Have Or to Be?*, he removed the chapter "Steps to Being" from the book in order to streamline it. In 1989, I then published this as the first posthumous volume with the title *The Art of Being*.)

At the time, Fromm had not yet known Nyānaponika Mahāthera for very long. They met in person for the first time in 1972 in Locarno when the Buddhist monk from Kandy in Sri Lanka visited his school friend, Max Kreutzberger. Nyānaponika had been born in 1901 as Siegmund Feniger, in the Hessian town of Hanau, and went to school in the Silesian city Königshütte with Kreutzberger, who later became Director of the Leo Baeck Institute in New York. In 1936, he emigrated to Ceylon to become a Buddhist monk. In his translations of Buddhist texts into German and English, he tried to bring the Buddhist teaching of "mindfulness" to people in the West.

For Fromm, Nyānaponika's role as a teacher was even more important than his role as a translator:

> I know of no other book about Buddhism comparable to *The Heart of Buddhist Meditation* in presenting with such lucidity the essential thoughts of this "atheistic religion" which appears so paradoxical to the Westerner. His style is always simple, but it is that simplicity which emanates only from a person who has mastered a complex subject so thoroughly that he can express it simply.
>
> *The Significance of Nyanaponika Mahathera for the Western World*, 1976b, p. viii

Nyānaponika introduced Fromm to mindfulness exercises, and from then on Fromm practiced them daily. Fromm had again found a master who wanted "to show the disciple the way to cure himself." This is the sort of teacher–student relationship that Fromm sought and continued to find throughout his life. The teacher should be a master. Masters teach by showing the ways that they themselves follow, finding a certain mastery in the process, and thereby experiencing the ways themselves as helpful. Someone who teaches without living what he teaches carries little conviction.

Fromm's own art of living illustrates a life of learning from masters. In his youth, the Frankfurt Rabbi Nehemia Nobel was a master for Fromm for several years. After Nobel's early death, Fromm's Heidelberg Talmud teacher Salman Baruch Rabinkow became an important guide and master. Both have been discussed here previously.

Although Fromm mentions her in his writings only sporadically, for several decades he found a very important master in Charlotte Selver (1901–2003). Born in Duisburg and trained by Elsa Gindler, she developed exercises for bodily and sensory awareness after her emigration to the USA (see Brooks, 1974).

Fromm met Charlotte Selver in New York in 1942 and studied weekly with her in hour-long sessions for an extended period of time. The goal of the exercises was to find an inner stillness and a sensory awareness of one's own body. With Selver's help, Fromm sought a direct encounter with his body—and found it. He was able to sense tensions and discover the psychological value of physical release as well as the increase in energy that this facilitated.

The effects of these exercises must have left a deep impression on Fromm and he practiced them with great discipline. To some of his patients and therapeutic training candidates he recommended that they might find a way to their psyche by working with their own body and taking lessons with Selver.

If Selver was an important master for Fromm's exercises in the art of living in the 1940s, beginning in the 1950s Daisetz T. Suzuki, Japanese Zen-Master and foremost messenger of Zen Buddhism to the West, took her place for the next two decades.

Fromm had already been familiar with Daisetz T. Suzuki and his writings before he moved from the USA to Mexico with his wife Henny in 1950. But only after Suzuki visited him in Mexico in 1956, followed by Fromm's meeting with him in New York, could Fromm sense "for the first time the feeling that I understood Zen, as if something had 'clicked,' as they say." And he immediately added in his letter to Suzuki: "I had some ideas of further application of some Zen principles to psychoanalysis, which I hope I can talk to you about when we see each other" (Letter to Suzuki, October 18, 1956).

Fromm's particular interest in Zen Buddhism and in Suzuki himself had to do not only with what Suzuki transmitted in terms of thoughts and ideas, but also with his own personally lived *experience of being one* with an object of perception—such as a rose or a cat. And indeed, while staying with Fromm in August 1957 to hold a seminar on "Psychoanalysis and Zen Buddhism," Suzuki would disappear for hours in the sprawling garden of the new house in Cuernavaca—down where the brook and the garden crossed paths, he would look at one of the cats of Fromm's wife Annis for hours on end.

Fromm understood the direct encounter and practiced it daily, not only in therapeutic work with patients but also in self-analysis and with the help of physical, meditation, and concentration exercises. The Zen Buddhist experience of oneness as he learned from Suzuki enabled Fromm to pose the psychoanalytic question of how a direct encounter with outer and inner reality is possible at all. He found the answer in a deepened understanding of the unconscious: only when the unconscious is the whole person can we become and be one in this mystical way.

> The unconscious is the whole man—minus that part of man which corresponds to his society. Consciousness represents social man, the accidental limitations set by the historical situation into which an individual is thrown. Unconsciousness represents universal man, the whole man, rooted in the Cosmos; it represents the plant in him, the animal in him, the spirit in him; it represents his past down to the dawn of human existence, and it represents his future.
>
> *Psychoanalysis and Zen Buddhism*, 1960a, p. 58

Zen Buddhism and psychoanalysis both offer ways of experiencing oneness with outer and inner reality in which the boundaries of the ego are overcome. Man can become one with an unconscious beyond space and time, without it resulting in a dissolution of the ego, as is the case in psychotic illnesses and pathological regressions.

Being with Suzuki was very fruitful for Fromm. As early as October 1956, Fromm presented Suzuki with the offer not just to return to Mexico for a few weeks but "to settle in Cuernavaca more permanently" (Letter to Suzuki, October 18, 1956). Fromm offered Suzuki the apartment in Cuernavaca that he and his wife used while their new house was being built at 9 Neptuno Street. Their move into the new house was planned for December 1, 1956. Fromm wanted to cover the housing costs for the 86-year-old Suzuki and his secretary, Mihoko Okamura, and to see to it that Suzuki could continue his teaching in Mexico.

Suzuki was only able to agree to a few weeks in the summer of 1957. At this time the now famous seminar "Psychoanalysis and Zen Buddhism" with Suzuki and Fromm as the main actors took place in the new house. Fromm's contribution, which shares the seminar's title, is without question the best piece he has ever written about the meaning of psychoanalysis (see *Psychoanalysis and Zen Buddhism*, 1960a).

The experiences of direct encounter with Suzuki continued in further meetings, but especially in the readings of Zen texts and in the daily practice of meditation. Fromm describes this in a letter to the more than 93-year-old Suzuki in Japan on April 29, 1964: "My wife and I read every morning either some Zen text or Meister Eckhart, so we are always in touch with you, even without letters."

As important as the direct encounters with masters of life were for Fromm, his own exercises and practice of the direct encounter remained essential. In general, Fromm tended to be skeptical when someone began to emulate a master of life and became his "disciple." When a psychoanalytic colleague and friend wanted to seek out Krishnamurti because of his troubles, Fromm wrote to him on March 19, 1975:

> As to Krishnamurti, I once met him and I have read some of his writings. I think he is an honest man and gives a kind of good abstract or basic idea of Indian philosophy and morals. Maybe it is a good thing to visit him but again I am afraid that it easily leads to becoming an adherent of Krishnamurti and that this becomes a resistance to one's active self-search.

The starting points for ways *toward* an encounter with others and oneself are for Fromm primarily ways *of* encounter with one's own self.

> To really relate is not a matter which depends primarily on the object. It is a faculty, it is an orientation, it is something in you, and not something in the object.
>
> *Dealing with the Unconscious in Psychotherapeutic Practice*, 1992g [1959]

After forty years of daily practice in encountering himself, Fromm states:

> I analyze myself every morning—combined with concentration and meditation exercises—for an hour and a half and I wouldn't want to live without it. I consider this one of the most important things I am doing. But it cannot be done without great seriousness and without giving it the importance which it has.
>
> *Therapeutic Aspects of Psychoanalysis*, 1991d [1974], p. 188

Anyone who has attempted to find ways toward a direct encounter with the self knows how difficult it is, how frequently one can head in the wrong direction of self-awareness, and how deeply one can delude and deceive oneself. How many "techniques" of self-awareness that bring happiness and redemption are for sale today? And how quickly we succumb to an inner resistance against desired change, if what has held us steady until now needs to be given up, because it may turn out to be a lifelong lie or an illusion! Before we can speak about ways of direct encounter with one's self, we must first clarify several of its preconditions.

Preconditions for an encounter with one's own self

With regard to the art of loving and the practice of learning it, Fromm writes, "The mastery of the art must be a matter of ultimate concern; there must be nothing else in the world more important than the art" (*The Art of Loving*, 1956a, p. 5). The same is true for the encounter with one's own self. The first requirement is therefore that one actually *wants* to encounter one's own self and seriously pursues this goal.

If one wants to be more than just mediocre, one must *want this one thing*, and this means, Fromm says in *The Art of Being*, "that the whole person is geared and devoted to the one thing he has decided on, that all his energies flow in the direction of this chosen goal" (1989a [1974–75], p. 31). In plain English, Fromm asserts not only that *daily* practice is required, but also that man must "*practice* discipline, concentration and patience throughout every phase of his life" (*The Art of Loving*, 1956a, p. 100).

Discipline here does not mean compulsiveness, but rather that man understands himself as a pupil (*discipulus*) who, rather than meditating whenever the mood or spirit hits him, knows that without practice nothing can be achieved, and therefore sets aside fixed times for practice and also practices in a disciplined way. Discipline is not imposed from the outside. It is essential "that it becomes an expression of one's own will; that it is felt as pleasant, and that one slowly accustoms oneself to a kind of behavior which one would eventually miss, if one stopped practicing it" (p. 101). *Concentration* excludes any other activity during its practice: "To be concentrated means to live fully in the present, in the here and now, and not to think of the next thing to be done, while I am doing something right now" (p. 103 ff.).

Concentration is still relatively easy to achieve when engaging in external or consciously executed activities. One cannot become inwardly still while listening to music or washing dishes. It is even more difficult to be concentrated when thoughts, psychic impulses, physical states of stimulation, or internal states of unease torpedo the stillness.

The ability to have *patience* is probably the prerequisite that causes the most problems today. In an era in which everything needs to happen quickly, everything is doable, and every small step forward needs to be observed and measured, patience has become a foreign word. In truth, however, "nothing serious is accomplished without great effort, patience, and honesty" (*Meister Eckhart and Karl Marx on Having and Being*, 1992s [1974], p. 139).

Certain prejudices and habits can make the resolve truly to want a direct encounter with one's own self more difficult. Such difficulties can be more easily overcome when those preconditions discussed previously have been met. Moreover discipline, concentration, and patience are important prerequisites that prevent defeat by *resistances* and *unconscious counterstrategies* that work against a direct encounter with oneself. Usually there are "good" reasons why we do not want or are unable to encounter ourselves directly—individual as well as social reasons.

An encounter can not only release energies and leave us more tranquil, relaxed, and at ease. It can also stir up anxieties and depressive states, lead to deep feelings of guilt or shame, cause conflicts to erupt with other people, or result in the surfacing of a powerless rage. The likelihood is actually very high that an encounter with oneself will be stressful, painful, and disillusioning because in most cases it means that one must let go of safeguards and defensive constructions, or that one must first be freed *from* something in order to be free *for* a direct encounter with oneself and others. By all means, one can bet on an internal resistance that works against movement toward one's own self and thus the resistance enables the invention of "good" reasons or rationalizations as to why this or that exercise is inappropriate, or that there is more important work to be done, or that this method does not go far enough, etc.

In this sense, *suffering*, a general unease or a not easily defined feeling of unhappiness and dissatisfaction with one's own situation, can be helpful in allowing one to be open to the effort of a direct encounter with one's own self. To suffer without "tangible" reasons in the form of illness, loss, or strokes of fate is not solely bad luck, although we experience it that way, but also an opportunity. This, of course, supposes that we associate such physical, mental, and intellectual states of suffering with an incorrect way of living. In that case, suffering can become a motivational force that even allows us to tread on rocky and anxiety-ridden paths.

Capacity for critique and readiness for dis-illusionment

Unlike most therapeutic methods, the art of living according to Fromm focuses above all on those obstacles in the way of a direct encounter that arise from nonproductive social character orientations. Such impediments rooted in character formations are usually not experienced as such, but rather, on the contrary, as legitimate forms of self-expression.

Whereas symptom formations are usually associated with suffering, character formations distinguish themselves by the way in which they are in tune with the self, that is, they are "ego-syntonic." Character formations can become annoying, for example, when someone needs to go around his car twice because of his compulsive character in order to check that all doors are actually locked, even though the car has a central locking system. The person in question, however, will not want to lose this character trait and will do everything possible to hold on to this "habit."

An individual's nonproductive character orientation already looks like an almost insurmountable obstacle because character formations usually do not produce any subjective suffering that might leave one ready to make radical changes. The social character orientation is even more challenging. The more certain character traits become dominant in a society or social milieu, that is, shared and enacted by a majority, the more they are experienced as normal and rational.

How could an ego-oriented person accept the threat of feeling even emptier inside with each shopping experience or cultural event, if he subjectively perceives the exact opposite, namely a deep sense of well-being in the shopping "paradise" or at IKEA, at the disco or at the Champions League after-party? And, for that matter, everyone else does the same thing and feels the same way. How can it be that what feels so good, the most normal, sensible thing in the world, allows one to become so inwardly impoverished?

Ways of behavior that are motivated by a social character orientation prove to be even more resistant to change than individual character traits because of their social prevalence and their acceptance within certain milieus. Any deviation from group-specific behavior is threatened with social isolation and stigmatization. When social norms are in question or even at stake, resistance usually tends to be correspondingly intense.

Fromm described this feature of behaviors determined by social character as the "pathology of normalcy" (*The Sane Society*, 1955a, pp. 12–22) and as early as 1944 spoke of a "*socially patterned defect*" (*Individual and Social Origins of Neurosis*, 1944a). The great "advantage" of social character formations lies in the way that they allow an individual "*to live with a defect without becoming ill*" (*The Sane Society*, 1955a, p. 16); on the contrary, a "flawed" art of living is socially sanctioned and declared a virtue.

To a sociological line of thinking focused solely on the success of society, which therefore deems normal what is socially acceptable, average, or practiced by the majority, Fromm counters:

> The fact that millions of people share the same vices does not make these vices virtues, the fact that they share so many errors does not make the errors to be truths, and the fact that millions of people share the same forms of mental pathology does not make these people sane.
>
> *The Sane Society*, 1955a, p. 15

With his concept of the "pathology of normalcy," Fromm emphasizes that all nonproductive social character orientations pose an obstacle to the art of living and to a direct encounter with one's own self. But because they can make a claim to social plausibility, their rationalizations present themselves as barely detectable ideologies. Anyone who questions them is attacked as a killjoy, know-it-all, old hippie, socialist, social reformer, incorrigible do-gooder, and is marginalized. While the authoritarian state feels threatened by the *disobedient* citizen, the "manufactured" state's lobbyists, consultants, and media feel threatened by *critical* contemporaries.

The *capacity for critique*, however, is for Fromm one of the most important preconditions for an encounter with others and oneself. Especially because suffering is foreign to social character orientations (present perhaps only when a character formation is no longer desirable or can no longer be enacted, because of a lack of money, profession, public or physical fitness), the capacity for critique with regard to one's own social success is indispensable.

> Critical thinking is the specific human ability. (...) Critical thought stands in the service of life, in the service of removing obstacles to life individually and socially which paralyze us.
>
> *Therapeutic Aspects of Psychoanalysis*, 1991d [1974], pp. 168–169

The ability to criticize cannot be circumscribed, but rather refers to all areas in which a pathology of normalcy is at work: in society, politics, the economy, religion, culture, one's own lifestyle, occupation, partnership, one's own ideas and values, etc.

> How can one be critical about the psyche of another person, about his consciousness if one is not at the same time critical about the general consciousness and the forces which are real in the world?
>
> p. 102

Nevertheless, socially critical insights assume a special significance to the degree that they result in a "conflict between the interests of most societies in the continuity of their own system as opposed to the interest of man in the optimal unfolding of his potentialities" (*The Dialectic Revision of Psychoanalysis*, 1990f [1969], p. 21).

The capacity for critique is almost always related to the *capacity for dis-illusionment*, that is, with a readiness to dispense with illusions about oneself and others, and with staging sentimental and illusionary realities. The word "dis-illusion" makes the emotional content clear: at stake is admitting to oneself that one has been relying on a self-inflicted or publicly demanded and promoted *illusion*, and that one is capable of renouncing it. This is indeed disenchanting, but also liberating. Otherwise:

> by not doing away with illusions one keeps alive circumstances which are unhealthy and which can only exist and continue because one makes oneself all these illusions.
>
> *Therapeutic Aspects of Psychoanalysis*, 1991d [1974], p. 169

Against this background, we see the many wrong turns that can be taken on the path toward an encounter with one's own self:

- Promotions of self-experience, well-being, self-awareness, healing, and therapy that can be acquired and consumed should be viewed skeptically, because they focus on what goes into people instead of what can come forth from them.
- Relying on techniques that promise they are learned easily, quickly, without effort, pain, disappointment, or loss suggests that no real change is desired.
- All opportunities that require identification with a teacher, spiritual leader, sage, or guru only strengthen the tendency to become dependent and to define oneself by outside icons, rather than exerting one's own powers.
- Self-experiences and meditation techniques that work with hypnosis and suggestion may lead to relaxation and temporary relief from symptoms, but do not necessarily lead to a mobilization of one's own powers.
- Exercises that do not lead to a strengthened perception of reality and a greater capacity to love often prove to be

counterproductive and lead to narcissistic preoccupations and self-satisfaction.

- Opportunities that offer to create a new inner man by focusing on spirituality and interiority, without acknowledging or wanting to change suffering related to political and social conflicts, block out the imprint of the social on the individual. For that reason, they can be reactions of resistance: one does not want to see how much one's own perception and striving for stability contribute to prevailing conditions.

- Likewise, all techniques and proposals that focus only on political activism and the application of psychological and social methods are to be viewed skeptically. They, too, can be reactions of resistance that prevent the experience of one's own powerlessness and helplessness.

- All practices and behavioral trainings whose only goal is negation, renunciation, or the liberation from something use human energy solely to be *against* something and thereby remain caught within a negation that they want to escape. Only by overcoming this state of being *against* through the awareness and practice of what one is *for* can one be liberated from the prison of asceticism and opposition, made free, and continue with the process of psychic growth.

Now that several preconditions for the encounter with one's own self have been clarified, I close with those ways that Fromm himself followed. He also proposed these more broadly as ways toward encounters with oneself and others.

Preparatory exercises

Ways *toward* direct encounter are ways *of* direct encounter. In the art of living according to Fromm, knowledge of, reflection on, or discussion about such paths cannot replace actually traveling on them. Only by treading the paths is the goal of direct encounter reachable. Fromm's own preferred pathways are:

- *Psychoanalytic therapy*, in which Fromm came into contact with other, until then unknown, aspects of himself through his patients.
- A *personal love relationship* in which Fromm exercised and practiced his ability to love as if it were a sensory capacity, so that a life lived without love would have seemed to him like a life with eyes that could not see.
- *Political action* for a society that makes human well-being its most important economic and social goal worldwide and which is able directly to face present threats; although this path of direct encounter has not been sufficiently emphasized here, all of those who encountered Fromm in person testify to his thoroughly political nature.
- *Personal connections* with friends, acquaintances, and scholars.
- *Self-analysis* and the preparatory exercises for an encounter with oneself.

The following focuses on this last pathway, which Fromm addressed predominantly in his posthumous writings. Karen Horney, with whom Fromm was close until 1943, published a book about self-analysis in 1942, which certainly also originated in discussions with Fromm and in each of their individual experiences of self-analysis. Fromm repeatedly mentions in letters that he does "his exercises" every morning and evening. In *The Art of Loving*, he recommends doing daily concentration exercises for at least twenty minutes in the morning, and ideally also in the evening before going to bed (1956a, p. 112). During my time as Fromm's assistant, he usually took an entire hour or even longer in the late morning to do his exercises and to analyze himself. Whenever Fromm speaks about exercises and self-analysis, he emphasizes the need for consistent activity.

> It is crucially important that it be done, like meditation and concentration, regularly and "not if one is in the mood." (...) Altogether the process of self-analysis should not have the character of forced labor, done in a grim mood of duty, yet necessary in order to reach a

certain goal. Quite aside from the result, the process in itself should be liberating and hence joyful, even though suffering, pain, anxiety, and disappointment are mixed in with it.

The Art of Being, 1989a [1974–75], p. 78

What does Fromm mean by *preparatory exercises*? Fromm practiced and recommended *concentration exercises* as an entry into self-analysis, as a way to become aware of oneself in a bodily state. One begins by sitting in a relaxed posture, with closed eyes. One should

> try to see a white screen in front of one's eyes, and try to remove all interfering pictures and thoughts, then try to follow one's breathing; not to think about it, nor force it, but to follow it—and in doing so to sense it; furthermore to try to have a sense of "I."
>
> *The Art of Loving*, 1956a, p. 102

The point of the *breathing exercises* is not to observe and think about one's breath, but rather to *feel* the process. "Once you begin to think, you are not aware of your breathing anymore." (*Therapeutic Aspects of Psychoanalysis* 1991d [1974], p. 179). Often,

> one will notice (. . .) that after a few seconds one stopped being aware of one's breathing and began to think of many often irrelevant things. To the degree to which one succeeds in concentrating on one's breathing, one is aware of the process of breathing.
>
> *The Art of Being*, 1989a [1974–75], p. 38

Another concentration exercise that Fromm practiced is a *movement exercise* that he learned from Charlotte Selver.

> Again one assumes the relaxed position and closes one's eyes. The hands are resting on one's upper legs (the posture one can see in the statues of the famous Abu Simbel sitting Pharaohs). One decides to raise one arm up to a forty-five-degree angle.
>
> p. 38

Usually, we move our arm with a purpose, in order to do something. In this exercise, the arm is raised, held, and then lowered very slowly, with eyes closed, in order to experience the process of movement only. When Tai chi chuan exercises are also understood as an art of movement, they too can be practiced as preparatory exercises. Fromm learned such exercises when he was older from Katya Delakova (see Delakova, 1991). For Fromm, concentration exercises lead directly to *meditation*, whereby Fromm distinguishes between two sorts of meditation. One, which also includes autogenic training, relies on autosuggestive techniques and in part attempts to induce light trance states in order to relax mentally and physically, as well as to gain a sense of one's own energy sources. Fromm could never really warm up to this meditation technique because of its autosuggestive aspects.

Fromm had a very different opinion of first the Zen Buddhist and later the Buddhist way of meditation, as he learned them from Nyānaponika Mahāthera (1973). "The main aim (...) is to achieve a higher degree of nonattachment, of non-greed, (non-hate) and of non-illusion" and to reach a *"maximum awareness* of our bodily and mental processes" (*The Art of Being*, 1989a [1974–75], p. 50). Such a meditation is "the highest activity there is, an activity of the soul, which is possible only under the condition of inner freedom and independence" (*The Art of Loving*, 1956a, p. 21).

"Mindfulness" is practiced not only in daily meditation, but "it is equally to be applied to every moment of daily living" (*The Art of Being*, 1989a [1974–75], p. 51). "The demand for optimal awareness of the processes inside and outside oneself" (p. 53) includes for Fromm mindful attention to social and political events.

There are many concentration exercises and methods of meditation such as "Yoga or Zen practice, meditation centered around a repeated word, the Alexander, the Jacobson, and the Feldenkrais methods of relaxation" (pp. 8–9), which Fromm came to learn about over the course of his life. What matters is that one practices that method that proves a helpful preparation for one's own self-analysis. For Fromm, there is no direct encounter with the self without self-analysis.

Self-analysis as a way of encounter

Someone who analyzes himself would like a different "depth experience" of himself that allows for drawing on his *own* bodily, psychic, and mental powers, and thereby enables his direct encounter with himself and the surrounding reality. He would like to be free of irrational fears and strivings, to uncover where he deceives himself by living a lie, and to let go of a stabilizing ego so as to gain access to hidden aspects of himself (*Psychology for Nonpsychologists*, 1974a, pp. 86–87).

Because every self-analysis means a descent into "the labyrinth of one's 'underworld'" (*The Dialectic Revision of Psychoanalysis*, 1990f [1969]), p. 78), Fromm found an introduction to self-analysis through a time-limited psychoanalysis of about six months helpful in treating pathological problems and dismantling strong resistances to the unconscious becoming conscious (see *The Art of Being*, 1989a [1974–75], pp. 66–69, and *Therapeutic Aspects of Psychoanalysis*, 1991d [1974], pp. 188–191). People with a weakened ego tend to want to replace real circumstances with their own wishful fantasy worlds, and often cling to a manufactured ego in their struggle to distinguish between inner and outer reality. For them, self-analysis can lead to a threatening loss of important survival strategies and foster a psychiatric illness.

Fromm draws attention to yet another danger:

> This experience—in whatever way it is produced, for example, through meditation, autosuggestion, or drugs—can lead to a state of narcissism in which nobody and nothing else exist outside of the expanded self. This state of mind is egoless inasmuch as the person has lost his ego as something to hold onto; but it can nevertheless be a state of intense narcissism in which there is no relatedness to anyone, inasmuch as there is no one, outside of the extended self.
> *The Dialectic Revision of Psychoanalysis*, 1990f [1969]), pp. 78 f.

In contrast to Freud and others who see mysticism as a regressive state, the mystics of the great religions are not concerned with a regressive "oceanic feeling," but rather a progressive oneness of the whole person from which the ego emerges strengthened, now capable of a more intensive direct encounter with external reality.

> Self-awareness, decreasing defensiveness, diminishing greed, and increasing self-activation may be steps toward enlightenment if they

are combined with other practices such as meditation and concentration, and if the person makes a great effort. "Instant enlightenment" with the aid of drugs, however, is no substitute for a radical change of personality.

p. 80

Here, too, we hear Fromm's reservations about drugs and autosuggestive methods. Self-analysis is about a deep change in personality, a change that emanates from the roots in the form of one's own growth-oriented powers.

The roads to the unconscious elaborated on in the first chapter (dreams, free association, parapraxis, and transference) are also the most important *methods of self-analysis*. For the Frommian art of living, behavior disorders that emerge from social character orientations and traits are an especially fruitful area for self-analysis. Discovering which nonproductive orientation is at work within someone enables a "revitalization" and the use of those productive forces of growth that have thus far been impeded or even thwarted.

Beyond this, Fromm offers an entire range of other possibilities. One is to observe one's own particular *symptoms* more closely:

> observ[e] certain symptoms such as feeling tired (in spite of sufficient sleep), or depressed, or angry, and then "feel around" what it was a reaction to and what was the unconscious experience behind the manifest feeling. (. . .) I mean by "feeling around" an imaginative "tasting" of various possible feelings until, if one has succeeded, a certain realization appears with clarity as being the root of the conscious experience of, say, tiredness.
>
> *The Art of Being*, 1989a [1974–75], p. 70

From there, one can also ask oneself about how this feeling might be familiar, in order to learn what the feeling represents.

Another sort of methodological approach is *autobiographical*. Fromm writes:

> Try to get a picture of significant events, of your early fears, hopes, disappointments, events that decreased your trust and faith in people, and in yourself. Ask: On whom am I dependent? What are my main

fears? Who was I meant to be at birth? What were my goals and how did they change? What were the forks of the road where I took the wrong direction and went the wrong way? (...) What is my image of myself? What is the image I wish others to have of me? Where are the discrepancies between the two images, both between themselves and with what I sense is my real self? Who will I be if I continue to live as I am living now?

p. 73

The phenomenon of a *screen memory* is well-known in therapeutic work: someone remembers a more or less significant childhood event and uses this conscious memory to cover a different, much worse, more shameful, hurtful, and frightening memory, and prevent it from becoming conscious. This phenomenon can also be observed with respect to the goals someone sets for himself: someone may have a conscious plan for his life which has the purpose of distracting from an unconscious, secret plan. Often the conscious plan serves to cover the unconscious one by virtue of its completely opposite goals. Consciously, a woman wants to become nothing like her mother, unconsciously, however, she does everything in order to identify with and remain connected to her.

Every self-analysis aims to uncover illusions about outer and inner reality. In putting an end to the illusion, it necessarily leads to a dis-illusionment. This process enables us to look directly at our own and others' reality, and activate our psychic capacity for growth. Self-analysis is therefore not an examination of conscience that allows one to lead a virtuous life, but rather an important part of the art of living that allows man to thrive.

For this reason, it is incorrect to think that "self-analysis increases the tendency for being occupied with oneself" (*The Art of Being*, 1989a [1974–75], p. 83). "Awareness refers not only to the uncovering of inner conflicts but equally to conflicts in social life that are negated and harmonized by ideologies (social rationalizations)" (p. 40). One cannot look within while remaining blind to the outside world. The critical capacity of the human mind is indivisible, or "the critical faculty of the human mind is one" (p. 40).

What can I know of myself as long as I do not know that the self I do know is largely a synthetic product; that most people—including myself—lie without knowing it, that "defense" means war and "duty" submission; that "virtue" means obedience and "sin" disobedience; that the idea that parents instinctively love their children is a myth; that fame is only rarely based on admirable human qualities, and even not too often on real achievements; that history is a distorted record because it is written by the victors; that over-modesty is not necessarily the proof of a lack of vanity; that loving is the opposite of craving and greed; that everyone tries to rationalize evil intentions and actions and to make them appear noble and beneficial ones; that the pursuit of power means the persecution of truth, justice and love; that present-day industrial society is centered around the principle of selfishness, having and consuming, and not on principles of love and respect for life, as it preaches. Unless I am able to analyze the unconscious aspects of the society in which I live, I cannot know who *I* am, because I don't know which part of me is *not* me.

pp. 77–78.

Self-analysis cannot shy away from what we are prevented from becoming conscious of for reasons of economic or social success. Only a consciousness critical in every respect, capable of distinguishing between social norms and what man needs to succeed, will not succumb to the pathology of normalcy. The pathology always consists of a socially dictated "healthy common sense" that impedes or thwarts man's well-being because it impedes or thwarts the psychic capacity for growth.

A direct encounter with others and strangers requires a direct encounter with one's own self. The daily practice of self-analysis is, according to Fromm's own experience, the best way to recognize the obstacles of what is socially repressed and rationalized as normality. This recognition paves the way for one's own conscious and unconscious productive forces of growth and their exercise, thereby confirming:

The more he develops his powers of love and reason; the more he acquires a sense of identity, not mediated by his social role but rooted in the authenticity of his self; the more he can give and the more he is related to others, without losing his freedom and integrity; and the more he is aware of his unconscious, so that nothing human within himself and in others is alien to him.

The Dialectic Revision of Psychoanalysis, 1990f [1969], p. 52

Encounters and their effects

Some readers may find themselves disappointed at the general nature of this encounter with the Frommian art of living through an introduction to Fromm's life and work. What very concrete steps for an art of living were described? Where are the specific directions that tell someone what to do? Such expectations must be disappointed, and not only because they reflect an ego-oriented Zeitgeist interested only in instructions for "manufactured" capacities and for which everything is only a question of the right technique. An introduction to an art of living that is interested in what underlies behavior and what consciously as well as unconsciously determines it cannot offer behavioral instructions. For Fromm, it was clear: "All I want—and am able—to offer are suggestions in what direction the reader will find answers" (*The Art of Being,* 1989a [1974–75], p. 8).

This book is about the direction, the orientation of those psychic forces that determines concrete behavior, what Fromm understood as character orientations. They inform human behavior in many ways, especially with regard to the question of whether man can further expand his human potential, above all his psychic capacity for growth, or whether he will allow it to atrophy. Because they indicate directions, the productive and nonproductive orientations can only be understood as alternatives to each other. One cannot go east and west at the same time. This does not preclude there always being a mix of nonproductive and productive orientations within an individual, so that he is sometimes pulled in one or the other direction (with much energy consumed by the resulting conflicts).

The direction in which someone is "pulled" by his own internal powers in his concrete behavior can be seen lastly in the *effects* that encounters with oneself, others, themes, and objects have. Based on its productive or nonproductive effects, we can recognize whether or not an encounter is conducive or detrimental to man's well-being. The most important effects should be touched on here in the conclusion (see Funk, 2005, pp. 221–225).

Every direct encounter has an *activating effect*: it leaves one feeling enlivened, awake, inwardly active, courageous, light-hearted, trusting, intensively aware and attentive, sensual, interested, engaged. One feels very present and time passes quickly. If a nonproductive orientation predominates, then an encounter has the *effect of passivity*: one feels bored, everything feels heavy and takes forever; without stimulation and entertainment, one feels empty inside or used up, without sensuality or sensual needs, unmotivated and tired.

Every direct encounter has an *energizing effect*: one feels full of life and a flow of energy, one wants to "overflow" and develops a need to give, to share, and to communicate. In contrast, if a nonproductive orientation predominates, then one observes that an encounter *consumes* energy; one feels spent, burned out, and exhausted; everything requires effort and leaves one feeling powerless and empty.

Every direct encounter has the effect of *strengthening empathy*: it promotes the ability to relate to people emotionally and with all five senses, to be sympathetic and empathic, curious and open to everything foreign and different about other people, cultures, and beliefs. If a nonproductive orientation predominates, then *distance* is created in every encounter: there is clarity only about the space one needs to allow for closeness; when interacting with what is outside of or foreign to oneself, feelings of anxiety or aggression surface, which in turn gives rise to reactions of superiority, distancing, or exclusion.

Every direct encounter has an *ego-strengthening effect*: it enhances the striving for autonomy, independence, and self-determination, allowing for awareness of one's own interests and individuality. One has a better sense of self in relation to reality, feeling on familiar and solid ground, more capable of awareness, suffering, frustration, and ambivalence. If a nonproductive orientation predominates, encounters increase the *incapacity to define one's own boundaries* and lead to symbiotic, controlling, or addictive dependencies. The capacity to differentiate between fantasy and the here and now, wishes and reality, mine and yours, decreases, at the same time the tendency to dissociate or settle conflicts by "either/or" grows.

Every direct encounter has an effect of *increasing creativity*: one feels more imaginative, intuitive, effervescent, free, spontaneous, and open for the new. If a nonproductive orientation predominates, we see a *lifeless effect*: an encounter leads to the desire for monotony, repetition, conformity, and imitation; one concentrates on reconstruction and wants to hold on to the experiences, preserve them, archive them, and reify them in behavioral instructions.

My encounters with Fromm, mentioned in the initial chapter, stand out in that I experienced them as "direct" encounters. In contrast to ordinary meetings, I recognized these "direct" encounters with Fromm by their effects. The resonance of these personal experiences with the central tenets of the art of living according to Fromm confirm that man's well-being depends on the practice of the productive orientation of his own powers. These powers must be liberated from social and individual instrumentalization in order to allow their full force as primary powers of growth to develop.

References

Bachofen, J. J., 1927: *Myth, Religion and the Mother Right*. Selected Writings, ed. by J. Campbell, Princeton (Princeton University Press), 1967.

Bauer, J., 2005: *Warum ich fühle, was du fühlst. Intuitive Kommunikation und das Geheimnis der Spiegelneurone*, Hamburg (Hoffmann und Campe Verlag).

Bauer, J., 2006: *Prinzip Menschlichkeit. Warum wir von Natur aus kooperieren*, Hamburg (Hoffmann and Campe Verlag).

Bauer, J., 2008: *Das kooperative Gen – Abschied vom Darwinismus*, Hamburg (Hoffmann and Campe).

Bauman, Z., 2000: *Liquid Modernity*, Cambridge (Polity Press).

Beck, U., 1992: *Risk Society: Towards a New Modernity*, Los Angeles (Sage); German original: *Risikogesellschaft: Auf dem Weg in eine andere Moderne*, Frankfurt am Main (Suhrkamp), 1986.

Brooks, Ch. V. W., 1974: *Sensory Awareness: The Rediscovery of Experiencing*, New York (The Viking Press).

Delakova, K., 1991: *Das Geheimnis der Katze. Eine Tänzerin weist Wege zum schöpferischen Üben*, Frankfurt (Brandes and Apsel).

Dornes, M., 1993: *Der kompetente Säugling. Die präverbale Entwicklung des Menschen*, Frankfurt am Main (Fischer Taschenbuch).

Dornes, M., 2006: *Die Seele des Kindes. Entstehung und Entwicklung*, Frankfurt am Main (Fischer Taschenbuch).

Dornes, M., 2012: *Die Modernisierung der Seele. Kind-Familie-Gesellschaft*, Frankfurt (Fischer Taschenbuch).

Ehrenreich, B., 2010: *Smile or Die: How Positive Thinking Fooled America and the World*, London (Granta Publications).

Fahrenberg, J., 2004: *Annahmen über den Menschen. Menschenbilder aus psychologischer, biologischer, religiöser und interkultureller Sicht*, Heidelberg (Asanger Verlag).

Fonagy, P., et al., 2003: *Affect Regulation, Mentalization, and the Development of the Self*, New York (Other Press).

Frankenberger, R., 2007: Die postmoderne Gesellschaft und ihr Charakter, in: R. Frankenberger, S. Frech and D. Grimm (eds.): *Politische Psychologie und Politische Bildung. Gerd Meyer zum 65. Geburtstag*, Schwalbach (Wochenschau-Verlag), pp. 167–187.

Freud, S., 1901: *The Psychopathology of Everyday Life*, in: *The Standard Edition of the Complete Psychological Works of Sigmund Freud*. Vol. 6, London (The Hogarth Press).

Friedman, L. J., 2013: *The Lives of Erich Fromm. Love's Prophet*, with assistance from Anke M. Schreiber, New York (Columbia University Press).

Fromm, E., 1929a: Psychoanalysis and Sociology, in: S. E. Bronner and D. M. Kellner (eds.), *Critical Theory and Society. A Reader*, New York and London (Routledge) 1989, pp. 37–39.

Fromm, E., 1932a: The Method and Function of an Analytic Social Psychology, in: *The Crisis of Psychoanalysis. Essays on Freud, Marx and Social Psychology* (1970a), New York (Holt, Rinehart and Winston), 1970, pp. 135–162. E-Book: https://www.overdrive.com/media/2045024/the-crisis-of-psychoanalysis

Fromm, E., 1936a: Sozialpsychologischer Teil, *Gesamtausgabe in zwölf Bänden* (GA), München (Deutsche Verlags-Anstalt/Deutscher Taschenbuch Verlag), 1999, Vol. I, pp. 139–187. E-Book: http://books.openpublishing.com/e-book/313964/

Fromm, E., 1939b: Selfishness and Self-Love, in: *Psychiatry*, Band 2 (1939), pp. 507–523; reprint in: E. Fromm, *Love, Sexuality, and Matriarchy*, New York (Fromm International Publishing Corporation), 1997, pp. 163–195.

Fromm, E., 1941a: *Escape from Freedom*, New York (Farrar and Rinehart). E-Book: http://www.openroadmedia.com/ebook/escape-from-freedom

Fromm, E., 1944a: Individual and Social Origins of Neurosis, in: *American Sociological Review*, New York, Vol. 9 (1944), pp. 380–384.

Fromm, E., 1947a: *Man for Himself. An Inquiry into the Psychology of Ethics*, New York (Rinehart and Co.). E-Book: http://www.openroadmedia.com/ebook/man-for-himself

Fromm, E., 1949a: The Nature of Dreams, in: *Scientific American*, New York (Scientific American Inc.), Vol. 180 (1949), pp. 44–47.

Fromm, E., 1949c: Psychoanalytic Characterology and Its Application to the Understanding of Culture, in: S. S. Sargent and M. W. Smith (eds.), *Culture and Personality*, New York (Viking Press), 1949, pp. 1–12.

Fromm, E., 1950a: *Psychoanalysis and Religion*, New Haven (Yale University Press). E-Book: http://www.openroadmedia.com/ebook/psychoanalysis-and-religion

Fromm, E., 1951a: *The Forgotten Language: An Introduction to the Understanding of Dreams, Fairy Tales and Myths*, New York (Rinehart and Co.). E-Book: http://www.openroadmedia.com/ebook/the-forgotten-language

Fromm, E., 1955a: *The Sane Society*, New York (Rinehart and Winston, Inc.).
E-Book: http://www.openroadmedia.com/ebook/the-sane-society

Fromm, E., 1955d: Remarks on the Problem of Free Association, in: *Psychiatric Research Report*, Washington (American Psychiatric Association), Vol. II (1955), pp. 1–6.

Fromm, E., 1955e: Psychoanalysis, in: J. R. Newman (ed.): *What Is Science? Twelve Eminent Scientists and Philosophers Explain Their Various Fields to the Layman*, New York (Simon and Schuster), pp. 362–380.

Fromm, E., 1956a: *The Art of Loving. An Inquiry into the Nature of Love* (World Perspectives Vol. 9, planned and edited by Ruth Nanda Anshen), New York (Harper and Row). E-Book: http://www.openroadmedia.com/ebook/the-art-of-loving

Fromm, E., 1960a: Psychoanalysis and Zen Buddhism, in: D. T. Suzuki and E. Fromm: *Zen Buddhism and Psychoanalysis*, New York (Harper and Row), 1960, pp. 77–141. E-Book: http://www.openroadmedia.com/ebook/psychoanalysis-and-zen-buddhism

Fromm, E., 1961a: *May Man Prevail? An Inquiry into the Facts and Fictions of Foreign Policy*, New York (Doubleday). E-Book: http://www.openroadmedia.com/ebook/may-man-prevail

Fromm, E., 1961b: *Marx's Concept of Man*. With a Translation of Marx's Economic and Philosophical Manuscripts by T. B. Bottomore, New York (F. Ungar Publisher Co.). E-Book: http://www.openroadmedia.com/ebook/marxs-concept-of-man

Fromm, E., 1962a: *Beyond the Chains of Illusion: My Encounter with Marx and Freud* (Credo Perspectives, planned and edited by Ruth Nanda Anshen), New York (Simon and Schuster). E-Book: http://www.openroadmedia.com/ebook/beyond-the-chains-of-illusion

Fromm, E., 1963f: Humanism and Psychoanalysis, in: *Contemporary Psychoanalysis*, New York (The Academic Press, Inc.), Vol. 1 (1964), pp. 69–79.

Fromm, E., 1964a: *The Heart of Man. Its Genius for Good and Evil* (Religious Perspectives, Vol. 12, planned and edited by Ruth Nanda Anshen), New York (Harper and Row). E-Book: http://americanmentalhealthfoundation.org/amhf-publications/

Fromm, E., 1966a: *You Shall Be as Gods: A Radical Interpretation of the Old Testament and Its Tradition*, New York (Holt, Rinehart and Winston). E-Book: http://www.openroadmedia.com/ebook/you-shall-be-as-gods

Fromm, E., 1967e: *Do We Still Love Life?*, in: *McCalls*, New York, Vol. 94 (August 1967), pp. 57 and 108–110.

Fromm, E., 1968a: *The Revolution of Hope: Toward a Humanized Technology* (World Perspectives, Vol. 38, planned and edited by Ruth Nanda Anshen), New York (Harper and Row). E-Book: http://americanmentalhealthfounda tion.org/amhf-publications/

Fromm, E., 1970b: (co-authored by Michael Maccoby): *Social Character in a Mexican Village: A Sociopsychoanalytic Study*, Englewood Cliffs (Prentice Hall), 1970. E-Book: https://www.overdrive.com/media/2044975/social-character-in-a-mexican-village

Fromm, E., 1973a: *The Anatomy of Human Destructiveness*, New York (Holt, Rinehart and Winston), 1973. E-Book: http://www.openroadmedia.com/ the-anatomy-of-human-destructiveness

Fromm, E., 1974a: Psychology for Nonpsychologists, in: E. Fromm: *For the Love of Life*, New York (The Free Press, Macmillan), 1986, pp. 66–87.

Fromm, E., 1974b: In the Name of Life. A Portrait through Dialogue, in: E. Fromm, *For the Love of Life*, New York (The Free Press, Macmillan), 1986, pp. 88–116.

Fromm, E., 1976a: *To Have Or to Be?*, New York (Harper and Row), 1976. E-Book: http://www.openroadmedia.com/to-have-or-to-be

Fromm, E., 1976b: The Significance of Nyanaponika Mahathera for the Western World. Foreword, in: B. Bodhi (ed.), *The Vision of Dhamma: Buddhist Writings of Nyanaponika Thera*, London (Rider), 1986, pp. vii–ix.

Fromm, E., 1977i: Interview mit Micaela Lämmle und Jürgen Lodemann: Das Zusichkommen des Menschen, in: *Basler Magazin*, Basel, No. 47 (24.12.1977), p. 3. E-Book: http://books.openpublishing.com/e-book/318094/

Fromm, E., 1979a: *Greatness and Limitations of Freud's Thought*, New York (Harper and Row), 1980. E-Book: http://www.openroadmedia.com/ greatness-and-limitations-of-freuds-thought

Fromm, E., 1980a: *The Working Class in Weimar Germany: A Psychological and Sociological Study*, edited and introduced by Wolfgang Bonß, London (Berg Publishers), 1984.

Fromm, E., 1980e: Mut zum Sein. Interview mit Guido Ferrari. E-Book: http:// books.openpublishing.com/e-book/318094/

Fromm, E., 1987a: Reminiscences of Shlomo Barukh Rabinkow, in: Leo Jung (ed.), *Sages and Saints*, Hoboken (Ktav Publishing House), 1987, pp. 99–105.

Fromm, E., 1989a [1974–75]: *The Art of Being*, ed. by Rainer Funk, New York (Continuum) 1993. E-Book: http://www.openroadmedia.com/the-art-of-being

Fromm, E., 1989b [1922]: *Das jüdische Gesetz. Zur Soziologie des Diasporajudentums.* Dissertation 1922, GA XI, pp. 19–126. E-Book: http:// books.openpublishing.com/e-book/310076/

Fromm, E., 1990d [1969]: On My Psychoanalytic Approach, in: E. Fromm, *The Revision of Psychoanalysis*, Boulder (Westview Press), 1992, pp. 1–9. E-Book: http://www.openroadmedia.com/the-revision-of-psychoanalysis

Fromm, E., 1990f [1969]: The Dialectic Revision of Psychoanalysis, in: E. Fromm, *The Revision of Psychoanalysis*, Boulder (Westview Press), 1992, pp. 19–80. E-Book: http://www.openroadmedia.com/the-revision-of-psychoanalysis

Fromm, E., 1990r [1966]: The War in Vietnam and the Brutalization of Man. Fromm's speech on the "SANE Garden Rally" on December 8, 1966. [So far not published in English.]

Fromm, E., 1991d [1974]: Therapeutic Aspects of Psychoanalysis, in: E. Fromm, *The Art of Listening*, New York (Continuum), 1994, pp. 45–193. E-Book: http://www.openroadmedia.com/the-art-of-listening

Fromm, E., 1991e [1953]: Modern Man's Pathology of Normalcy, in: E. Fromm, *The Pathology of Normalcy: Contributions to a Science of Man*, New York (American Mental Health Foundation), 2010, pp. 15–80. E-Book: http://americanmentalhealthfoundation.org/toc.php

Fromm, E., 1991h [1974]: Is Man Lazy by Nature? in: E. Fromm, *The Pathology of Normalcy: Contributions to a Science of Man*, New York (American Mental Health Foundation), 2010, pp. 109–146. E-Book: http:// americanmentalhealthfoundation.org/toc.php

Fromm, E., 1992d [1961]: Modern Man and the Future, in: E. Fromm, *On Being Human*, New York (Continuum), 1994, pp. 15–31. E-Book: http:// www.openroadmedia.com/on-being-human

Fromm, E., 1992e [1937]: Man's impulse structure and its relation to culture, in: E. Fromm, *Beyond Freud: From Individual to Social Psychoanalysis*, New York (American Mental Health Foundation), 2010, pp. 17–74. E-Book: http://americanmentalhealthfoundation.org/toc.php

Fromm, E., 1992g [1959]: Dealing with the Unconscious in Psychotherapeutic Practice, in: E. Fromm, *Beyond Freud: From Individual to Social Psychoanalysis*, New York (American Mental Health Foundation), 2010, pp. 83–122. E-Book: http://americanmentalhealthfoundation.org/toc.php

Fromm, E., 1992h [1975]: The Relevance of Psychoanalysis for the Future, in: E. Fromm, *Beyond Freud: From Individual to Social Psychoanalysis*, New

York (American Mental Health Foundation), 2010, pp. 123–147. E-Book: http://americanmentalhealthfoundation.org/toc.php

Fromm, E., 1992m [1962]: A New Humanism as a Condition for the One World, in: E. Fromm, *On Being Human*, New York (Continuum), 1994, pp. 61–79. E-Book: http://www.openroadmedia.com/on-being-human

Fromm, E., 1992s [1974]: Meister Eckhart and Karl Marx on Having and Being, in: E. Fromm, *On Being Human*, New York (Continuum), 1994, pp. 114–170. E-Book: http://www.openroadmedia.com/on-being-human

Fromm, E., 2000f [1979]: Encretien d'Erich Fromm avec Gerard D. Khoury. Interview with Erich Fromm, in: E. Fromm, *Revoir Freud. Pour une autre approche en psychoanalyse*, Paris (Armond Colin), 2000, pp. 149–180. Partial publication of the English original in: *Fromm Forum* (English Edition), No. 12 (2008), pp. 33–40, and in *Fromm Forum* (English Edition), No. 13 (2009), pp. 5–13.

Fromm-Reichmann, F., 1954: Transcription of an interview, originated on 1954. Partially published in: A.-L. Silver, Frieda Fromm-Reichmann – Reminiscences of Europe, in: A.-L. Silver (ed.), *Psychoanalysis and Psychosis*, Madison (International Universities Press), 1989, pp. 469–481.

Funk, R., 1978: *Erich Fromm: The Courage to Be Human*, New York (Crossroad/Continuum), 1982. PDF: http://www.fromm-gesellschaft.eu/index.php/de/publikationen-blog/buecher/204-the-courage-to-be-human

Funk, R., 1983: *Erich Fromm. Mit Selbstzeugnissen und Bilddokumenten*, Reinbek (Rowohlt Taschenbuch Verlag).

Funk, R., 1992: Der Humanismus in Leben und Werk von Erich Fromm. Laudatio zum 90. Geburtstag, in: *Wissenschaft vom Menschen – Science of Man*, Jahrbuch der Internationalen Erich-Fromm-Gesellschaft, Vol. 3 (1992), Münster (LIT-Verlag), pp. 133–151.

Funk, R., 2000: *Erich Fromm – His Life and Ideas. An Illustrated Biography*, New York (Continuum International), 2000; Softcover edition, 2003.

Funk, R., 2000a: Psychoanalyse der Gesellschaft. Der Ansatz Erich Fromms und seine Bedeutung für die Gegenwart, in: R. Funk, H. Johach, G. Meyer (eds.), *Erich Fromm heute. Zur Aktualität seines Denkens*, München (Deutscher Taschenbuch Verlag), pp. 20–45.

Funk, R., 2002: Destruktivität als Faszination und Folge ungelebten Lebens Erich Fromms Verständnis der Nekrophilie, in: M. Zimmer (ed.), *Der 11. September und die Folgen. Beiträge zum Diskurs nach den Terroranschlägen und zur Entwicklung einer Kultur des Friedens*, Tübingen (self-published), pp. 57–89.

Funk, R., 2003: Was heißt "produktive Orientierung" bei Erich Fromm?, in: *Fromm Forum*, No. 7 (2003), pp. 14–27.

Funk, R., 2005: *Ich und Wir. Psychoanalyse des postmodernen Lebens*, München (Deutscher Taschenbuch Verlag).

Funk, R., 2005a: Erleben von Ohnmacht im Dritten Reich. Das Schicksal der jüdischen Verwandtschaft Erich Fromms, aufgezeigt anhand von Dokumenten und Briefen auf dem Weg in die Vernichtung, in: *Fromm Forum*, No. 9 (2005), pp. 35–79.

Funk, R., 2006: Love in the Life of Erich Fromm. A Biographical Afterword, in: E. Fromm, *The Art of Loving*, New York (HarperCollins—Harper Perennial Modern Classics) 2006, Appendix, pp. 9–22.

Funk, R., 2009: *The Clinical Erich Fromm. Personal Accounts and Papers on Therapeutic Technique*, ed. by Rainer Funk, Amsterdam and New York (Rodopi Publisher/Brill).

Funk, R., 2011: *Der entgrenzte Mensch. Warum ein Leben ohne Grenzen nicht frei sondern abhängig macht*, Gütersloh (Gütersloher Verlagshaus).

Funk, R., 2012: "Was machen die Medien mit dem Menschen? Sozialpsychologische Beobachtungen," in: *Fromm Forum* No. 16 (2012), pp. 25–34.

Funk, R., 2014: The Unbounded Self: The Striving for Reconstructing Personality and Its Clinical Impact, in: *International Forum of Psychoanalysis*, Vol. 23 (No. 3, 2014), pp. 144–150.

Funk, R., 2017: "Die Bedeutung der Liebe im Werk von Erich Fromm," in: *Fromm Forum* No. 21 (2017), pp. 38–49.

Goldman, N., 1969: Reminiscences of Shlomo Barukh Rabinkow, in: L. Jung (ed.), *Sages and Saints*, Hoboken (Ktav Publishing House), 1987, pp. 105–107.

Hardeck, J., 2005: *Erich Fromm. Leben und Werk*, Darmstadt (Wissenschaftliche Buchgesellschaft).

Horney, K., 1942: *Self-Analysis*, New York (W. W. Norton and Co.).

Hüther, G., 1999: *Die Evolution der Liebe*, Göttingen (Sammlung Vandenhoeck).

Hüther, G. and Spannbauer, Ch. (eds.), 2012: *Connectedness: Warum wir ein neues Weltbild brauchen*, Bern (Huber).

Lifton, R. J., 1993: *The Protean Self. Human Resilience in an Age of Fragmentation*, New York (Basic Books).

Maccoby, M., 1999: *The Self in Transition: From Bureaucratic to Interactive Social Character*. American Academy of Psychoanalysis, May 14, 1999. Digital: http://www.maccoby.com/Articles/SelfInTransition.shtml

Marx, K., 1968: *Ökonomisch-philosophische Manuskripte aus dem Jahre 1844,* in: Marx-Engels-Werke, Ergänzungsband I, Berlin (Dietz Verlag), pp. 465–588. English trans. in: E. Fromm, *Marx's Concept of Man.* With a Translation of Marx's Economic and Philosophical Manuscripts by T. B. Bottomore, New York (F. Ungar Publisher Co.), 1961.

Nyānaponika Mahāthera, 1973: *The Heart of Buddhist Meditation,* London (Rider & Co.), 1962, New York (Samuel Weiser), 1973.

Rabinkow, S. B., 1929: Individuum und Gemeinschaft im Judentum, in: *Die Biologie der Person. Ein Handbuch der allgemeinen und speziellen Konstitutionslehre,* ed. by Th. Brugsch and F. H. Lewy, Vol. 4: *Soziologie der Person,* Berlin und Wien (Urban und Schwarzenberg) 1929, pp. 799–824.

Rosa, H., 2016: *Resonanz. Eine Soziologie der Weltbeziehung,* Berlin (Suhrkamp).

Schröter, M., 2015: Neue Details über die psychoanalytische Ausbildung von Erich Fromm (und Frieda Fromm-Reichmann), in: *Fromm Forum,* No. 19 (2015), pp. 112–115.

Schulze, G., 1992: *Die Erlebnisgesellschaft. Kultursoziologie der Gegenwart,* Frankfurt am Main (Campus).

Sennett, R., 1998: *The Corrosion of Character,* New York (W. W. Norton).

Index

www.ingramcontent.com/pod-product-compliance
Ingram Content Group UK Ltd.
Pitfield, Milton Keynes, MK11 3LW, UK
UKHW020735280225
455688UK00012B/661